THE
2020
BOARD

C000205672

Published by
LID Publishing Limited
The Record Hall, Studio 204,
16-16a Baldwins Gardens,
London EC1N 7RJ, UK

524 Broadway, 11th Floor, Suite 08-120,
New York, NY 10012, US

info@lidpublishing.com
www.lidpublishing.com

A member of:

Business Publishers Roundtable

www.businesspublishersroundtable.com

All rights reserved. Without limiting the rights under copyright reserved, no part of this publication may be reproduced, stored or introduced into a retrieval system, or transmitted, in any form or by any means (electronic, mechanical, photocopying, recording or otherwise) without the prior written permission of both the copyright owners and the publisher of this book.

© Pedro Nueno, 2019
© LID Publishing Limited, 2019
First edition published in 2016

Printed in Great Britain by TJ International
ISBN: 978-1-912555-41-3

Cover and page design: Caroline Li
Illustrations from *The New Yorker*

THE 2020 BOARD

Pedro Nueno

LONDON   NEW YORK   SHANGHAI
MADRID   BARCELONA   BOGOTA
MEXICO CITY   MONTERREY   BUENOS AIRES

CONTENTS

FOREWORD

Over the course of my career, it has been my privilege to be a member of many company boards. As a professor of business administration, I have always been interested in variety. Whenever I thought I could contribute something of value, I have accepted directorships across a miscellany of industries, and at companies of widely varying sizes, ranging from listed corporations to family-owned businesses in the US, Europe, Latin America and Asia.

Over the years, I have also lectured and taught in programmes aimed at company directors. At many companies, I learned so much that I felt rather than them paying me, it almost would be fairer for me to pay them. And with many of the programmes on which I have taught, I have had that same sense of having learned at least as much as I imparted; this makes me feel thankful to the students and to the rest of the faculty–often drawn from other world-class business schools.

These experiences have prompted me to write this book, in an attempt to put the best ideas I have learned into some sort of order, from the standpoint of the changes that companies are undergoing in the decade 2010-2020: technological progress in general and, especially, digitalization, globalization of the world economy, and huge markets opening up to everyone. These shifts are compelling companies to make far-reaching changes at great speed.

The board of directors can, and ought, to be key to the leadership of a business: encouraging the emergence of a robust strategy, achieving optimal value creation, treating employees with the respect they deserve as people, nurturing the company's own culture – its values, its corporate citizenship – and, above all making sure that everything is done ethically and legally in all markets in which the company operates. These are the topics I propose to address in this book.

As an alumnus of Harvard Business School in the US and a professor at IESE Business School in Barcelona, the case-study method forms part of my mindset. As in my earlier books, I have tried to construct situations that resemble some of my experiences – although of course I adapt them slightly – to illustrate the way some directors behave and how company boards approach certain issues.

Finally, as a long-standing reader of *The New Yorker*, which for many years has discussed both the theory and practice of company boards, I am an enthusiast of its delightful cartoons on the subject. The editors of that publication have graciously allowed me to use some of their cartoons to illustrate this book.

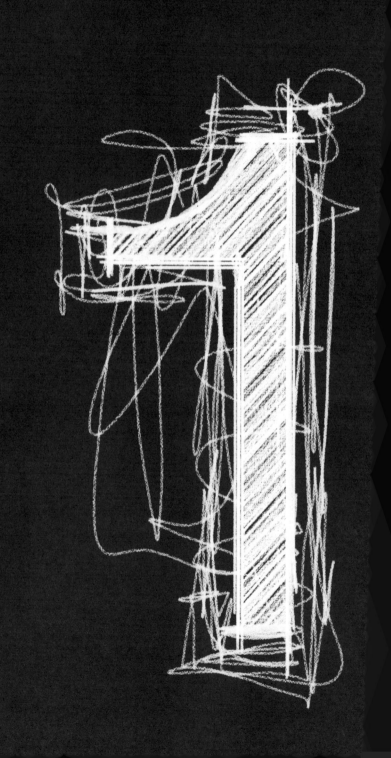

INTRODUCTION

The economic downturn that began in 2008, the explosive development of the information society, the rising significance of ethical issues in the business world and its environment – particularly the political sphere – and phenomena such as increasing globalization, technological evolution and, especially, digitalization, have triggered a worldwide debate about the role of company boards. In many cases, it is clear that boards have been blindsided by business issues or misconduct by senior managers. The concept of 'governance' means framing rules, adopting them, putting them into practice and making sure they are followed.

Business involves the use of a number of models. Some are highly structured, such as the balance sheet, the income statement and the cash flow statement. Others are less quantitative and hence less tightly structured:

- Strategy
- Organizational schemes and people management (levels, areas of responsibility, assessment and remuneration policies, in-house career track, training)
- Operational management (technologies, processes, equipment, sites, logistics, procurement)
- Commercial management (marketing, advertising, sales)
- Finance and relations with stakeholders in capital markets, banks, investment banks, potential investors (venture capital, private equity, business angels, stock exchange)
- Innovation and its related research and development – and control of the whole, collecting information promptly and accurately and turning it into reports that allow for close monitoring by managers and using the internal audit function to ensure that the reports depict the reality and that the reality is within the rules the company must abide by (the law, industry standards, existing patents, commitments to third parties).

It is up to the board to ensure all these processes flow correctly and efficiently. In one sense, the board is an intermediate organ: company executives report to the board and the board is accountable to share-holders. However, it functions independently of either.

One of the classics of management literature is Alfred Sloan's *My Years with General Motors* (1963).[1] In the 20th century, General Motors was long considered the best company in the world: innovation in the au-tomobile industry, rapid growth, international presence, brand man-agement and so on. Alfred Sloan was the chief executive officer (CEO) of General Motors from 1918 to 1941 and a member of the board for 45 years, from 1918 to 1963. This period witnessed several reces-sions, the Second World War, spells of strong growth, the emergence of tough competition both domestically and internationally, and ma-jor technological progress.

The company's success, however, had a lot to do with Alfred Sloan's effective management approach, which he sets out in his book. The key decisions in the life of the company – ranging from foreign in-vestment to handling a cutthroat strike – were made by an internal structure with the features of a governance body that today we would categorize as something between the 'executive committee' and the 'shareholders' meeting'.

Turning to the retail industry in that same period, *History of Macy's of New York* by Ralph Hower,[2] a leading faculty member at Harvard Business School, shows that the main decision-making and oversight functions were performed by what Hower calls the "board of opera-tions" and the "advisory council." Over the course of the 20th century, the institution of the board of directors did make some progress, but perhaps less so than the other management bodies mentioned above.

Since the start of the 21st century, however, company boards and corporate governance have become important issues of debate. The business world has clarified that corporate governance can, and must, stimulate value creation, make companies stronger and open doors to

"*I, too, hate being a greedy bastard, but we have a responsibility to our shareholders.*"

contributing to the community. This is an end-to-end concern: it triggers change, creates relevant knowledge and leads to the framing of new rules and standards. Professor Jay Lorsch, a leading business mind, now at Harvard Business School, has researched company boards thoroughly and one of his latest books explores what the future might hold for them.[3] I have worked alongside him in programmes aimed at board members and it is likely that some of the ideas proposed in this book are the outcome of that partnership.

RAIL BASIC PROVIDERS (RBP)

Patrick Collins was approached by an acquaintance, who was the chairman of the board of Rail Basic Providers (RBP), a European company that supplies railway construction materials – chiefly rails and sleepers. Patrick was offered a directorship. RBP, a firm with more than 50 years of history behind it, was now a subsidiary of a major infrastructure group that had been state-controlled for many years until it was privatized in the 1970s.

Patrick found that RBP had a robust balance sheet, acceptable performance, moderate growth, and a low profile. He tried doing some research into the industry, but there was not much out there in the way of information. He was surprised to see that one of the references on the recommended reading list was a book by one Charles P Cotton, *Manual of Railway Engineering,* published in 1874.[4] This was a detailed set of instructions on building, regulating, and gaining government approval for railway construction projects in the UK and Ireland. Having read this dense tome, he realized that most of the innovation and change undergone by the railway industry was unrelated to the tracks themselves. RBP was largely dependent on earnings made on the maintenance of a large number of railway lines.

As an engineer, Patrick had worked at an infrastructure construction firm, which mostly engaged in building motorways, ports, tunnels, and airports, but had occasionally built sections of railway. On the face of it, he was comfortable with the technical side of the job. He had held a number of directorships and accepting this new appointment looked like the smart thing to do: there would be only six board meetings a year, each requiring just a two-hour flight to another city, and plenty of timing alternatives were available.

At his second board meeting, Patrick got a surprise. The supporting information was supplied at the meeting itself and was, in any event, very scarce. The chairman of the board was also RBP's CEO. The other board members included two RBP executives, the executive president, two directors of RBP's parent company, and the former CEO of RBP, now retired – like Patrick, he was characterized as 'independent'. So there were eight board members in total.

The strangest thing about it was that very little was said at meetings about RBP itself. There would first be an overview of the latest data (usually several months old), then a few highlights – almost invariably about the parent company, only sometimes with a relevance to RBP's order book. Discussion would turn from the business to the wider economy, and from the economy to politics, and gradually the meeting became a sort of free-flowing chat show, bearing no relation to RBP. Meetings would start at 12 noon and break for lunch at 1.30pm. But very often the directors would arrive late and the meeting would become much the same thing as lunch.

Directorships were well paid and Patrick didn't know what to do. If he tried telling them this wasn't a board meeting but a chat show, they might feel offended. It was clear to him, though, that this didn't make sense in 2015 and that he shouldn't be there—out of a sense of professionalism, but also because it might damage his reputation. At a later meeting, he resigned on the pretext that he was overstretched by an excessive workload. He thanked the other directors for having appointed him and offered to provide them with any assistance they might need in future.

Unfortunately, Patrick Collins's experience is not exceptional. Quite a few company boards operate like RBP's. Patrick's story revolves around a board that doesn't work as it should. Some members think of their directorship as a reward for services rendered to the company during their former tenure as executives. Others see it as a part of their current roles as company managers. And a few independent directors regard it as a form of remuneration for the prestige they bring to the company with their track record, or for the recognition attached to having held public office.

This sort of attitude may be more widespread at government-controlled companies and their equivalents, where technological, financial, and sales risks are low, as seemed to be the case at RBP. Yet a comfortable position could also serve as the springboard for taking controlled risks to widen the business in a meaningful way – even where this involves diversification. The company board could stimulate this kind of mindset instead of falling back on routine and red tape. What's more, the unedifying example set by a chat-show board often leads to talent loss. In 2015, one thing is clear: what goes on in the board is known throughout the company.

Sometimes a board appointment is a form of remuneration. It can be a way of giving people a post-retirement, end-of-career reward, thanking them for their length of service or some special contribution they might have made; a way of padding out a senior executive's compensation when the company pays less than the going rate. Sometimes, part of the compensation is the mere prestige of holding a directorship. Still, although boards of this sort continue to exist, there is a strong trend towards adding value from the corporate governance perspective.

In the following chapters, I shall look at different ways in which a company board can become more professional, in keeping with our times. We shall discuss the tried-and-tested knowledge we now have in this field, addressing the 'reality' through case studies based on real-life situations – which I have adapted to preserve anonymity and bring out the key points.

THE ORGANIZATIONAL STRUCTURE OF A BOARD OF DIRECTORS

The role of a company board is hard to describe in a succinct statement. However, we could say that the purpose of the board is to oversee the company as a whole, so as to guide it toward sustained, long-term value creation. It's important for board members to have a thorough knowledge of the company, but it's impracticable for the board to address every area in detail. Hence, the first crucial challenge is to supply the board with the right kind of condensed information. It's also very difficult for the board to have a comprehensive grasp of the industry in which the company operates, or to know everything about present and potential competitors and their specific strengths and weaknesses. Nevertheless, the board should be able to position the business within its industry and evaluate the consequences.

Looking inward, it is not feasible for the board to have a highly detailed awareness of all the technological and innovation-driven issues that might, or might not, impinge on the business, the processes involved in producing the company's goods and services, or the potential evolution of key technologies. There are limits, too, to the board's knowledge of the company's executives and key persons, in so far as the organization might be structured into different business units, each with its own management, sales, technology, operations, human resources, and finance people; or the business might have an international reach, with large organizations in different regions.

Despite this, the board ought to be able to draw judicious conclusions on the vital aspects of all these concerns and to evaluate accurately the company's position in each area as satisfactory, requiring improvement, or clearly deficient.

To achieve this and to do its job, the board must have the necessary capabilities and be supplied with the right information.

COMPOSITION OF THE BOARD

There are many kinds of director. Some are on the board to represent stakeholders, while others bring special skills and capabilities (although this side can be supplemented elsewhere). Some directors act on behalf of owners or are owners themselves. This is particularly frequent in family-owned businesses, where some board members hold a percentage in the company. But there are also many listed companies where a major shareholder – a bank, an investment fund, or a powerful individual investor – wants to have one or more people on the board to act in his or her interests.

Likewise, it is very frequent for senior executives – the chairman, the CEO, vice chairman, and other senior officers – to be appointed to the board. Senior executives may also be company owners or at least hold a significant stake. Occasionally, where senior managers are partly remunerated in the form of shares, they may acquire a large enough ownership interest to be entitled to a seat on the board.

Another key category of directors are 'independents': professionals with a strong track record and no significant ties to the company's owners or executives. The idea is that independent directors are not linked to the company through their management experience (they don't carry the baggage of friendships, psychological ties, company routines, or corporate culture in relation to peers, government bodies, or the wider community).

An independent directorship does not usually entail much in the way of dedication, remuneration, or prestige. Typically, an independent director has retired comfortably, has sold off his or her business, or is a reputable former professional (lawyer, consultant, executive, academic) whose career now consists of advising companies in a board-member capacity.

Irrespective of the categories to which he or she belongs, an effective director should perform the distinctive functions of corporate governance separately to the grounds of his or her appointment: ownership interests, involvement in management, or advisory membership. It can be hard for proprietary directors to consent to decisions that might involve an erosion of the interest they hold or represent (for example, entry into a fund, far-reaching bank refinancing, or entry of a new shareholder who contributes a key market, technology, or international presence).

Likewise, it can be tough for an executive director to concur with a board majority decision that thwarts an initiative that he or she has set in motion.

Finally, an independent director may be reluctant to support a decision that would involve his or her departure from the board, such as the sale of the company. It is not unusual for proprietary and executive directors to be overly attached to the business. They tend to resist the insight that, over the long term, the company will be unable to achieve the international expansion it needs because it has fallen behind the rest of the industry and hence the best move from the point of view of extracting value is to sell it off. It is in cases like this that an independent director can play a decisive role – although if the business is sold, he or she is likely to be dropped from the board.

BOARD COMMITTEES

To ensure the board functions properly, it is usual practice to set up board committees, made up of sub-groups of directors, to address specific issues in more depth. This provides the rest of directors with an assurance that those points are being correctly handled. The most commonly used forms of board committee are the audit committee and the appointments and remuneration committee.

AUDIT COMMITTEE

Many organizations employ internal auditors, who conduct an ongoing, detailed verification of financial and business reporting. The audit committee ensures the company's internal audit function and checks that the accounts that reach the board accurately reflect the company's financial position and performance. If the company does not have an internal audit unit, the audit committee works with the company's statutory auditors, who update their reports in accordance with the committee's guidelines.

The audit committee is often chaired by an experienced, independent director with thorough knowledge of the company and strong financial expertise. If the company has an internal auditor, it is often good practice to give him or her a place on the committee.

The audit committee's schedule of meetings usually ties in with the schedule of board meetings and often meets just before or soon after the board to assist with directors' logistics and make the process more efficient. Overall, the audit committee usually meets three to five times a year. Its schedule includes preparing for statutory audits, entering into related discussions with the auditors and submitting conclusions to the full board. Over the course of a year, the committee focuses on facts and events that might impact the financial statements and that accordingly require decision making by management and the board: for example, depreciation of the currency of a country in which the organization is present or unethical conduct by a key account manager.

APPOINTMENTS AND REMUNERATION COMMITTEE

The appointments and remuneration committee oversees organizational changes, especially those affecting senior management positions and remuneration levels and schemes. For second- and third-tier management positions, the committee examines general proposals (for example, pay rises, performance-related pay, and bonuses). For top-tier

*"As board members, we need to speak with one voice.
I'm suggesting Donald Duck."*

management, the committee takes a case-by-case approach. Crucial assistance is provided by the head of human resources and, in many cases, the CEO.

The current trend is to split this committee into two – appointments on one hand, remuneration on the other. This is one way of preventing the problem mentioned earlier: making an appointment as a sort of remuneration, which might give rise to organizational setbacks.

OTHER COMMITTEES

Some boards set up other committees – which may be temporary or permanent – to deal with issues that are particularly important for the company. The most frequent of these other committees is the strategy committee, which keeps a close watch on the implementation of existing plans and reformulates strategy on an ongoing basis. If the company is largely tech-based, the strategy committee may focus on technology and even be called the "technology committee."

Clayton Christensen, a professor at Harvard Business School and one of the leading scholars in the field of innovation, has stressed that some large companies face special challenges in this domain and this is when it is appropriate to stimulate innovation at the highest corporate level.[5] Other companies set up a body known as the "disruptive commission" or "disruptive council" that includes people from outside the organization. The purpose of the disruptive commission is to encourage discussion about issues that might crucially affect the economy, society, or the industry in which the company operates. The debate is open-ended and it is only at the closing stages that attention turns specifically to the evolving environment's potential impact on the company.

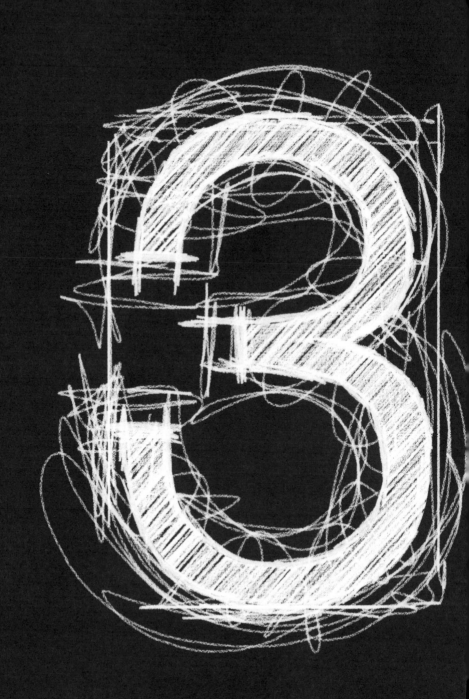

INFORMATION
FOR THE BOARD

The directors should receive specific information needed for a board meeting approximately a week in advance. One of the basic pieces of information they require is the company's financials as they stood at a recent date: balance sheet, income statement, cash flow, and sales. These data should be shown in relation to budgeted figures. If the organization is divided into separate business units, the accounts should be broken down accordingly. The figures may, of course, differ slightly from the actual final situation, because it is only after the financial year-end and the statutory audit that the final picture becomes available. But for an effective function of the board, it is vital to receive and rely on recent and complete data that closely reflects reality.

If there are major shifts in the accounts that might have a special impact – debt restructuring, a large investment, devaluation of a currency in which the organization conducts a large proportion of its business – the board should be supplied with financial information specifically concerning that impact.

The board may also have to look at other matters arising in the life of the company. For instance, the departure of a key executive; a dispute with labour or legal implications; an impending strike due to failed wage negotiations; or a round of layoffs; the threat of patent litigations; a sharp hike in the price of a key commodity; and so on.

Some issues may be external to the company but nonetheless important, such as the merger of two competitors (which are thus able to exert greater pressure on the market and achieve economies of scale in production, marketing, and advertising). A significant technological innovation introduced by a competitor might transform the industry, with real consequences for the company; the board would have to engage in a prompt discussion about the potential impact and decide how to react.

It is particularly important for the board to be well acquainted with the management team, especially top-tier executives: those heading up each of the company's functional areas and business units. One of the best ways for the board to get to know the key people is to invite them to board meetings at which issues affecting their roles will be coming up for discussion. It is common practice to ask the executive to make a presentation, briefing directors on the topic at hand and setting out his or her own views. The executive can then join the ensuing discussion. At later board meetings, he or she may be invited back to provide a brief update on steps taken, results achieved, and progress made in the areas under his or her responsibility.

Another way to keep directors informed is to ask them to visit key company locations: production sites, research and development centres, or foreign subsidiaries. If the firm produces consumer goods such as food, it is an interesting exercise to look at the products on a supermarket shelf or at the grocers surrounded by competing labels.

Many companies tap into the potential of special events for generating information (major conventions and conferences) and by hosting a side event of their own for a selection of middle and senior managers, clients and suppliers and, of course, board members. This sort of occasion can enrich the company's culture, encourage interaction among the company's own people and draw on interesting ideas generated by experts or competitors. For the directors, gatherings like this can be a unique opportunity to glean information about the business, and some companies even arrange to hold a board meeting during, just before, or after the wider event.

Another major information source for the board is consultancy firms, especially those that have a specific unit or team of experts focusing on the company's own industry. Consultants can supply the board with key knowledge about the industry and help organize and present it in a way that optimizes board performance. A wealth of board-related

"Leak this against my wishes."

material helps raise the standard above the average of the industry or, if the company has lagged behind, at least catch up with the average.

Confidentiality is vital. Some firms are so concerned about this issue that they do not supply directors with highly sensitive information in the form of hard copy or electronically. Instead, the information is disclosed at the board meeting itself, either screened in the course of proceedings or provided in written form, subject to its being returned. These extreme measures are not unusual.

Directors generally dislike this approach because it seems to assume that they will leave board papers lying around in the airport business lounge or recklessly share them with their email contacts. Other confidentiality procedures include providing information over password-protected servers or as hard copy only. Common practice in 2015 is to distribute board information online, except for particularly sensitive issues, for which the data is shared at the meeting itself, sometimes only on screen.

IMAGINARY AUTOMOTIVE COMPONENTS (IAC)

One Saturday last June, Frank was up early in his Amsterdam townhouse. He sipped a cup of freshly brewed coffee while his laptop booted up. A stack of emails had piled up in his inbox. Attached to one was the supporting information for the next meeting of the board of the French firm, Imaginary Auto Components (IAC), which was coming up the following Wednesday in Paris. He clicked on 'print' and carried on processing his inbox: sifting, sorting, mostly deleting.

He stapled together the 30-odd sheets of material for the IAC board meeting and thought, "I'll read this on the way there." On Wednesday he'd have to be out of the door by 5 am to catch his flight to Paris. With the plane landing at 8 am, he would have more than enough time to get to IAC before 9:30 am, when the meeting was scheduled to start. In excellent shape at the age of 72, Frank had a great deal of board-level experience. He had been on the IAC board for five years now, so an hour and a quarter in a business-class seat would be plenty of time for breakfast and catching up on IAC's facts and figures. IAC would send a driver to pick him up, so he would have at least another 30 minutes, if needed.

It was a sunny day and he took a walk with his wife Rebecca. "What's on your mind?" she asked. Frank realized he hadn't spoken a word. He was thinking about IAC. He decided that, when he was back at home, he would block out some time to look at the latest figures and make up his mind about a thing or two. Frank was happy about his contribution to the IAC board so far, but had been feeling a little less comfortable lately.

IAC had grown strongly in the first half of the 2000s, doubling its revenue to €500 million. The company was owned by the three founding shareholders. They had managed the business effectively, each playing to their strengths: one of them had focused on the industrial and product side, another on marketing and sales, and the third on finance. In 2008, the sales-focused shareholder sold his stake to Material and Component Supplier (MCS). In the months following the new industrial partner's entrance, the other two founders left the management of the firm to their teams, but retained their ownership interests.

At this time, the board comprised the two founders, the son of one founder and the daughter of another, two senior executives who had acquired part of the outgoing founder's stake, MCS's appointee, and two independent directors. Frank was a close friend of the key contact at the investment bank that had advised on the industrial partner's entry into the company. It was the investment banker who had recommended that the board be set up. He had sketched out the basics of the board and had proposed Frank as a director.

An industrial engineer, Frank had trained in management at Nyenrode in his native Netherlands and at other European schools, such as IESE, and US schools like Harvard. He spent the early years of his career at Philips and then moved to Volkswagen in Germany. Next, he worked at a big international consultancy firm and then gradually retired while taking up various directorships.

In 2009, he was offered a place on the board of IAC. He was interviewed by the two founding shareholders and the chairman of MCS. They made a formal offer and he accepted. He was fairly certain that his investment banker friend – who had the ear of MCS and who'd let him know that he'd gotten the job – had put in a good word for him. Yet Frank regarded himself as an independent director; he was sure that if the other two shareholders had pushed back against his appointment, MCS wouldn't have tried to impose him on them. And when the chairman of MCS nominated Frank as a director, he made it clear that he was expected to act as an independent.

Back from his stroll around Amsterdam, Frank went to his home office and browsed the IAC board papers. He remembered that, in early 2009, when the board was set up, there was almost no reliable information about the company to be found. Clearly, the business was doing well, the company was making money, and sales were on the up. But the figures were unreliable and did not reflect any clear strategy, nor was it easy to put them in relation to the industry (suppliers, clients, competitors). The board did excellent work, slowly building up the foundations needed for professional management: they developed a strategy, mapped it onto an organizational structure, created a framework of accounts (balance sheet, income statement, cash flow), made forecasts, revised unrealistic ratios, and acquired in-depth knowledge of the industry and IAC's position within it.

To get their hands on all these management tools and key data, the board – and the two independent directors especially – pushed hard to bring in good consultancy firms. The founding directors and their children – who of course supported them – were reluctant at first, because the consultants were quoting what seemed to them excessively high fees. They felt it was throwing money away. But finally the data provided by the consultancy firms enabled the board to get a clear picture of IAC's situation, its position in the industry, and helped them manage the company more effectively.

IAC had been a successful venture for the founders, who had spotted a good opportunity to supply car manufacturers with a complex subset of parts that called for highly skilled labour, good technical specialists, and wide flexibility. These things were hard to organize for a large car manufacturer and IAC was in a position to plug the gap. By continuing to improve its basic products, the company had retained its clients. And because the particular components that IAC supplied accounted for only a small part of the carmakers' total procurement, it was not a priority for them to reduce prices, so the company was able to keep an attractive profit margin.

But as more – and better – information emerged about the company and the industry, Frank began to worry about IAC's future. IAC's main competitors were large multinationals. Geographic proximity to manufacturers such as Renault and Peugeot, cemented by the friendly relations between the founders of IAC and those companies' procurement managers, had led to steady sales at attractive prices. They had also made some inroads into supplying German manufacturers like Volkswagen and, for a brief period, Audi. But they had never closed a deal with Mercedes or BMW.

In an increasingly globalized environment, IAC had gradually lost market share. Frank was not getting any real answers to his questions. The forecasts being shown to the board were based on past revenue growth and historic margins. But from 2008 to 2012, the reality had been far worse than expected. The company invariably blamed the economic downturn and its impact on the automobile market. Its reluctance to venture beyond France was very strong, even though the data showed that IAC could sell its products in the US, Latin America, Eastern Europe, China, India and Korea. This would involve a minor investment in each overseas location, setting up a barebones facility to adapt the goods to the local market, arrange distribution and cater to clients' specific requirements.

Moreover, in 2013, IAC's competitors had encroached on what had previously been IAC's own patch, partly because IAC had been unable to accommodate a spike in demand. It annoyed Frank that he would find out about these things months after they happened and only after asking detailed questions prompted by the discrepancies between forecast and actual performance data.

The industry-wide figures he'd seen for the first quarter of 2014 showed that car sales had picked up strongly almost everywhere across the board. Frank turned to his file of earlier board papers to retrieve IAC's performance data for the first quarter of 2013 and compare it with the data of the first quarter of 2014. He found that, year on year, IAC's revenue had in fact dropped. More worrying still, year-on-year earnings had declined more steeply than revenue. But detailed information was lacking on the various clients, markets (weak export results), and competitors.

To gain a handle on the problem, he needed more complete data. He had a hunch that concentrating on the French market was dampening IAC's performance and letting the competition gain ground even within France. The company's likely reaction had been to retain business by lowering prices. Frank knew that, at least as things stood at the last board meeting in mid-February 2015, there were no product innovations in the pipeline.

Almost without realizing it, he'd now spent two hours on the 30 sheets of board papers and his IAC data file. He'd noted down the questions he wanted to ask to gain a better understanding of the state of play. Summoned to lunch, he came downstairs with a furrowed brow.

"What's wrong?" asked Rebecca. Frank realized that, at the next board meeting, he ought to make the suggestion that it might be best (and urgent) for the current shareholders to sell off IAC. The company was clearly incapable of the innovations and global rollout that would be required to return to growth. IAC's current position would probably still be attractive, however, for some of its competitors, particularly those that still didn't have a foothold in France.

Frank smiled at his wife and decided that, after lunch, he would prepare for the next board meeting with the goal of persuading the three shareholders to sell their stakes. He was pleased that by pushing for more information about the company and its context over the past few years, he had obtained sufficient data to arrive at a sensible estimate of the value of IAC. Perhaps he should talk to his investment banker friend? The idea would be to get the proposal to sell accepted and then have his friend engaged to advise on the transaction.

Back in his office, Frank mulled over his ideas. Was it the right thing to do to propose that his friend handle the sale? It seemed reasonable: he was well acquainted with the company and its shareholders and he had successfully managed the sale of a holding to MCS. He had also nominated him, Frank, as a director, and Frank believed he had done some good work there. It reflected well on his ethics that the deal would most likely entail his departure from the board with no severance pay from the shareholders. So he was convinced that his proposal was in the shareholders' best interests and that he needed to nudge them toward a prompt decision, because IAC would only lose value as time went on. There was nothing in it for him.

Frank sensed that the IAC management team was unable to run the company effectively in an increasingly competitive, globalized, and technology-intensive environment. Out of remorse, rather than bad faith, the managers were being stingy with the data, lest the company's decline become too obvious. This made it harder for the directors to do their job. As they had been insufficiently aware of what was going on in the industry, they hadn't had the information they needed to recommend effective action. But now Frank's conclusion was clear. They had to sell, and quickly. The business was at risk of losing value very rapidly. If his recommendation were rejected, Frank thought he ought to resign from the IAC board immediately. He was also confident that his friend, the investment banker, would make a special effort with IAC and was therefore the right man to push the deal through. Frank knew that his conduct on the IAC board had been impeccably ethical. It was his duty to suggest the sale of the company even if this would involve his own departure from the board and his record as a director comfortably placed him in the 'independent' category.

Frank is a good example of an independent director. He spent six years struggling to get IAC's management to supply the right information to the board. He detected gaps–some of them probably intentional–and had them filled. Now he had to put forward a proposal that would almost certainly never be heard by the management: to sell the business. Yet Frank was sure this was the best way out and, what's more, it was urgent.

If the deal went through, Frank would probably have to leave the board and he would not get anything out of it. It hadn't been easy for him to find out what was happening in the company and in the wider industry. The management team had tried to conceal the decline of the business and its lack of traction outside France, despite the swift and unstoppable globalization of the car industry. Getting hold of the best information had been a real fight. Frank even had to resort – in the face of the proprietary directors' resistance – to using independent consultants. His role on the board had not been an easy

"You stay and answer the phone."

one, and almost without realizing, he had spent more time on it than is normally expected of a non-executive director. The board had never set up any committees. But a properly formed audit committee would have helped enhance the available information. Maybe this was one of the things that Frank ought to have tried to get going.

One alternative that Frank could have suggested was to replace the management team. That course of action would have been rejected by the executive directors, but might have found support with the owners. However, Frank believed that, at this late stage, there was neither time nor resources to implement the exhaustive and painstaking changes that IAC required.

We might question whether getting hold of the right information should really have taken as many years as it did. Frank had been rowing against the current, because some of the directors, feeling comfortable with the state of affairs and believing it was sustainable over the long term, preferred to ignore the reality. All the same, five years to gain a clear picture seems a long time. If the decision to sell had been proposed a year earlier, it would have been just as reasonable, and the value of the business would have been higher.

BOARD SIZE, MEETINGS, AND PREPARATION

NUMBER OF DIRECTORS

How many directors should be on a company board? If the firm is a leading name, or makes the news because of a merger or takeover, or because it is in trouble, the number of board members is often highlighted in the media, together with the directors' names and pictures. In our information age, there's no such thing as confidentiality. Over the years, the average number of directors has decreased. Research from the past 20 years shows boards were comprised of more than 20 members. Boards of 14 or 16 directors are still common, but my bet is that the average figure will approach eight or nine as 2020 grows closer.

The speed at which information spreads, and the boldness of the media in publishing it, means that anyone can now get information on those on a board, how long they have sat on it, how much they earn, which the other boards they sit on, and any other relevant details. This has placed pressure on the workings of boards and reduced director numbers, also driving those whom remain on boards to more rigorous standards of professionalism.

At the same time, company boards have been targeted by a wide range of 'soft laws' and guidelines, recommended internal rules and new statutory provisions for their functioning, accountability, and transparency. Today, a directorship comes with a considerable burden of responsibility. The notorious Enron affair may have triggered heavier regulation of corporate governance. That burden is now a fact, exacerbated by globalization, which requires multinational organizations to comply with rules prevailing in many different jurisdictions.

So, contrary to what many might think, sitting on a company board is no picnic. A director must have a thorough understanding of the business, ensure the company does well and brings good news, prevent irregularities and complies with laws and regulations that may constrain what members of the board can do (for example, conflict of interest rules and non-compete rules).

"Our stock just went up ten points on the rumor that I was replacing you all with burlap sacks stuffed with straw."

NUMBER OF BOARD MEETINGS

How many board meetings should there be in a given year? The number of meetings seems to be evolving from an average of eight to approximately ten a year. Excluding the summer break and winter holiday months, that's about one meeting a month. However, this is not always the case and at some companies the board meets only six – or just four – times a year. Such infrequent meetings make it difficult for directors to understand the business properly and monitor it closely.

How long should a board meeting last? In order to achieve a thorough follow-up of the company's affairs, an effective grasp of the business and focused attention on the key issues, the directors ought to dedicate a considerable length of time to all meetings. Each director must set out his or her point of view and argue for it. There may be serious disagreements. In order to guide executive actions effectively, the conclusions reached must be consistent and specific. Clearly, this requires time. At many company board meetings, the expectation is for it to take about six hours, but occasionally, a board meeting may call for a whole day; this is generally flagged up in advance.

The customary procedure is to circulate a schedule of board meetings in the course of the previous year. By September at the latest, the dates are set for all the following year's meetings. With all directors present, the chairman proposes a schedule and adjustments are made to fit in, as far as possible, with any previous arrangements the directors may have.

NUMBER OF WOMEN DIRECTORS

Another important consideration for company boards in 2015 is the number of women on the board. The current proportion of women directors on company boards in Europe and the US is approximately 23%. A related and interesting question is: how many women go into business? A proxy for that figure might be the answer to the question: how many women get MBAs? A review of admissions data from the world's leading business schools indicates that the proportion of women in current MBA programmes is close to 30%. That percentage is on the rise; 25 years ago, the proportion was only around 20%. This suggests that, if at that time 20% of entry-level management candidates were women, it would make sense to see a similar percentage of women in the upper tiers of corporate management today.

At many companies, however, the proportion of female board members falls far short of 20%. Clearly, there are many women out there who are strongly qualified and widely experienced – including those in corporate governance roles – who would make good candidates for directorships. With an objectively professional view, we can expect that, by 2020, at least a third of board members should be women.

How long should a director hold office? Most companies appoint their directors for terms of four to five years, but these appointments allow for at least one re-election. This makes for a total tenure of eight to ten years. Historically, some directors have held office for more than 20 years; but looking toward 2020, there appears to be a trend toward faster replacement.

As a director, it's hard to get to know a company well in less than a year, so there needs to be a balance in the rate at which the board is replaced. In a board of eight to ten people, the ideal rate would be to replace one member a year. This would ensure both continuity and renewal. If the chairman is also the CEO, he or she may hold office for a longer period if the management proves effective and performance is strong. Other directors – independent ones in particular – could rotate every eight to ten years, with changes made to the board in step with strategic development.

"*This is goodbye, gentlemen. I have met another board of directors, and we have fallen in love.*"

DIRECTOR TRAINING

What qualifies a person to become a director? In answering this question, we should look to the 2020 horizon. We are moving toward it with an eye on opportunity, amid a process of globalization and digital transformation that is impacting the entire value chain. Directors should have an innovative and entrepreneurial mindset, while complying with prevailing laws and regulations and making increasingly meaningful contributions to corporate social responsibility. The board should be able to address all these themes, making sure that its scope is comprehensive and that it does its job well, moving in the right direction and creating value. These requirements are clearly making increasing demands in terms of the training, qualifications, and skills that board members must bring to the table.

It makes sense, for instance, that a company producing high-tech medical diagnostic equipment should have a physician on the board. That doctor should also have business acumen, however and the other directors should have sufficient medical knowledge to understand the company's products and markets. Fortunately, today there is a rich array of courses that train professionals in business basics and corporate governance and boards are becoming increasingly aware of the importance of ongoing training for directors.

Another key theme of our times is internationalization. Directors should have an international track record: maybe they've worked at companies with an international reach, have managed firms or subsidiaries in other countries, or have held directorships at global organizations. An effective director should feel at ease in the face of international challenges and be able to guide and encourage the company to take the global stage.

BOARD SECRETARY

The board secretary is becoming an increasingly significant role. First, he or she takes care of logistics, such as calling meetings and sending the supporting documents. He or she liaises with the company for any clarification or to request further information that a director may need (for example, contact with the audit committee, confirmation of an unexpected datum, clarification of possible errors, or suggestions for addressing a given item on the meeting agenda in more depth).

Second, the board secretary draws up the meeting minutes, recording the main points raised by directors and the decisions made. The secretary is often in charge of screening the board's decisions from a legal standpoint. This is particularly important at listed companies. In some cases, the board secretary's role is virtually outsourced to a corporate governance expert at a law firm.

The meeting minutes also engage the problem of confidentiality. Anything written down and circulated might, through carelessness or bad faith, end up in the wrong hands. Should the board's decisions on the most sensitive issues affecting the company be included in the minutes? Can we ask directors to download the minutes from a password-protected server? Some board secretaries are artful enough to draw up minutes that are intelligible only to board members, by taking for granted that the reader is perfectly aware of the key points and options discussed. Sometimes, however, when an issue is highly sensitive, at the following meeting the minutes are read out by the secretary and – if thought appropriate – adopted by the directors present, but not subsequently circulated.

HEALTHY FOOD SUPPLIERS (HFS)
Healthy Food Suppliers (HFS) was a firm engaging in the distribution of health foods. These high-quality products emphasized health-related aspects (sugar content, vitamin content, brands with a reputation

for quality and wholesomeness and so on). The goods were sold at supermarkets with demarcated health areas, dedicated health food retailers, and generalist distributors offering health foods in proximity to over-the-counter drugs. In 2015, this family business was owned in four equal shares by two brothers and two of their cousins. The executive chairman was a professional. He was neither a shareholder nor a member of the family. The parents of the current owners had appointed him about ten years previously, on the occasion of the transfer of the shares to the next generation, as agreed within the family.

In 2014, Ralph, one of the shareholders, attended a leading business school in the US and took a course on corporate governance. It made a big impression on him. He persuaded the other three shareholders to create a board of directors. Ralph suggested they contact the professor who had taught the corporate governance course and ask him for assistance in setting up a professional and effective board.

The professor welcomed them into his office and asked them whether they had brought the company accounts. They had not. The professor asked about the headline figures, but the shareholders were mostly unable to reply. They did not work at the company themselves. They had entrusted the running of the business to their finance director, who supplied them with the audited accounts for each year before April of the following year. They did, at least, remember the top-line figure; they knew the company was profitable and relatively unburdened by debt. They were unable to be more specific. They had a good grasp of the products and the major clients.

Of the four shareholders, one of them had a PhD in engineering and another was a doctor of medicine and their work was in their respective fields. The other two had graduated in economics and were running fairly successful real estate businesses.

The professor found that they expected him to set up the company's board of directors unaided. All four shareholders had understood that it was not enough to have a good manager. There had to be a board to supervise him, to help him keep up, or even improve, the company's performance and step in if required – for instance, if the manager should fall ill.

Thinking about what the real state of the company might be, the professor guessed a board of eight people would probably suffice. Ideally, the board should be composed of the four owners, the executive chairman and the finance director, with two further directors recruited from outside. The four shareholders would be proprietary directors, the two in-house people would be executive directors, and the two new people, independent directors. The professor suggested this structure. The shareholders insisted that he, himself, accept one of the independent directorships.

The professor knew a large number of professionals then holding board appointments at various companies and more than one of them would have been a good fit for HFS. But in order to recruit someone who would be unquestionably independent, he thought it would be best to engage the services of a headhunting firm specializing in selecting board members. This would be consistent with the decisions made so far and would also provide an avenue for discussing the structure of the board with a team of experts. Despite the cost, this suggestion was well received by the four owners.

The professor offered to act as board secretary at the first few meetings, after which he would look to have that position filled by a lawyer in the law partnership from which the company usually sought advice.

The professor seems to have done a good job, although remaining off the board and advising the family as an outsider might have better preserved his independence. As a director, he was affected by most board-related decisions. For example, the first board arrangement may not have worked effectively and its structure might have needed to be rethought; another example, rotating family-member directors, recruiting a new director, removing an existing one and so forth. It may have been a good idea to commission a professional search for the other independent director, too, and to use this experience to obtain expert input – in the form of the headhunters' reactions, questions, and comments – on the process of setting up the board.

If the professor had stayed off the board, the full range of professional reactions surrounding the search for two independent directors would have provided a richer experience and added more value. His role as adviser to the family had been key and the position of independent director was somewhat inconsistent with this. His proposal to hold the board secretary position, however, was sensible, since it was likely that no one inside the company had the requisite expertise and awareness of the risks faced by the company, particularly in the health field.

In July 2015, the European Central Bank criticized Spanish banks for supplying insufficient information in their board minutes. It is likely that the major moves decided on by banks and reported by the media were not in the minutes, but obviously must have been discussed at board meetings. Let's return to the issue of confidentiality, which is key to implementing an ambitious strategy swiftly and with entrepreneurial drive.

BOARD
PROCEEDINGS

GROUP DYNAMICS

According to Ram Charan – a former professor at Harvard Business School who has dedicated much of his academic career to the subject of company boards – for a board to work effectively, it must have the right group dynamics.[6] Ram says that directors must build an efficient and effective working group. He would often quote the famous CEO and president of the board of General Electric, Jeff Immelt: "The boardroom has to be a place where every voice is heard. Our meetings are very open. Directors can interact with anybody, at any time." Michael Garo,a highly successful serial entrepreneur, with more than 30 companies to his name, would no doubt agree.[7]

The conversation at a board meeting requires directors to be suitably prepared, and this, in turn, calls for accurate and complete information that gives them a good understanding of the company and its industry. The board will find that achieving a dialogue leading to a strategic decision, which may involve major investments and affect a large number of employees and shareholders who place their trust in the company, is no simple matter.

TYPES OF DIRECTORS

To illustrate the difficulty of getting the board to engage in progressive discussion, let's identify some 'extreme' types of directors.

THE SELF-APPOINTED 'EXPERT':

The 'expert' used to serve on the board of a very large company, let's say ABC Global Corporation. Quite often, she will say things like: "Whenever this kind of issue has arisen for the board of ABC Global Corporation, we have always decided to do such-and-such." ABC Global Corporation is such a big name that the 'expert' director believes her contribution carries weight due to ABC's prestige alone.

"For God's sake, Edwards. Put the laser pointer away."

Of course, if the matter in hand closely resembles a situation that a former director of that big company has experienced during her tenure, it would be valuable for her to mention that, "When faced with this issue previously, we would have done such-and-such" (provided confidentiality is preserved).

THE 'I HAVE A QUESTION' DIRECTOR:

When a conversation involves 16 people, it's sometimes difficult to get a word in edgeways. One way of interrupting the flow and being heard is to ask a question that is more or less relevant to what the current speaker is saying. For instance, if two board members are engaging in a discussion about the commercial approach to be taken in a troubled market like Brazil – which, despite its great potential, is set to decline in 2015 – the "I have a question" director can jump in by saying: "Excuse me, I have a question. Do we still have that distributor in Brazil who also operated in other Latin American countries?"

Once he has his foot in the door, he doesn't bother to wait for the answer to his question, but carries on with what he meant to say all along: "In our industry there are several distributors who are firmly entrenched in Latin America, and since we don't have a permanent office there perhaps we should make an alliance with a powerful distributor…"

THE 'CHATTERBOX':

Some directors seem unaware that they are droning on. Quite often, there is very little content in what they say. It takes them forever to get to the point, if there is one. They seem to be thinking aloud. This sometimes happens with people who used to hold a senior executive position or public office, and during their mandate became accustomed to taking the floor without being interrupted, despite not saying anything of real substance. They can speak quite loudly, which makes it hard for other directors to raise a different topic or make a relevant point.

THE 'SILENT TYPE':

The silent type doesn't say much. The advantage for her is that, as soon as she signals that she is ready to speak, she is quickly given the floor and everyone listens. The downside for her is that, because she speaks so rarely, what little she does say had better be good. But a quiet, knowledgeable, and well-prepared director can be useful in guiding and focusing the discussion at crucial points, and helping to move the meeting forward.

THE 'TECHNICAL GUY':

On some boards there is one director who has specially mastered one of the key topics affecting the company. In the face of swift techno-logical change and its effect on business, it may be beneficial to have a director who knows about technology to devote 20 or 30 minutes – not more – at the start of the meeting to update the rest of the board about recent developments that might touch on the industry or the company specifically.

For instance, take the board of a pharmaceutical company, one of whose competitors has acquired a biotech firm. The conventional drug treatment for a given disorder may be about to give way to a biotech-nology approach. If that is on the company's horizon, many of its areas, including research and development, production, marketing, and sales would be affected and the board should stimulate and oversee a crucial strategic shift.

THE 'CONNECTED' DIRECTOR:

The 'connected' director enters the boardroom, places his laptop on the table and boots up to read the board papers on screen. In the pro-cess, he takes a little time out to browse his email and fire off a couple of replies that, he thinks, can't wait. Next to his laptop, he plonks down an iPad so that he can continue to read emails while at the same time glancing at the board papers on the laptop. On the other side of the laptop he has his phone, which he's switched to 'vibrate'.

"Huh? Oh, yeah—I do."

During the meeting, he listens, takes part and uses his laptop to take notes. Once in a while his phone starts buzzing. He picks up, finds out who's calling and sometimes whispers, "I can't speak right now, I'm at a board meeting. I'll call you later." But sometimes he'll say, "Yes, put them through." He stands up and goes to a corner of the boardroom believing no one can hear him, when in fact he's raising his voice, as many people do when they speak on the phone.

By the end of a six-hour meeting, the "connected" director might have spent one of those hours reading and replying to emails, answering and making phone calls and texting back and forth. The worst thing is that he is blithely unaware of the fact that his to-ing and fro-ing in and out of the meeting annoys the other directors, particularly the chair.

MANAGING THE MEETING

Some of the examples above may be a little extreme, but within a group of ten board members, it is likely that there will be several who at least partly resemble one or more of the 'types' described. To ensure the group makes progress and arrives at a range of decisions to guide the company toward strategic value creation, there must be one or two people who steer the meeting in an effective way. This role ought to be the main duty of the board chairman. The board secretary can often help, by reminding directors of the items on the agenda, monitoring the progress made in relation to the time remaining and asking for clarification for the purpose of the supporting notes of the board minutes.

LUXE FOOD EUROPE (LFE)

Mathieu Pomper, chairman of the board of Luxe Food Europe (LFE), a manufacturer of high-quality, lavishly designed biscuits and chocolates, opened the board meeting in early 2015 by announcing to directors that the plan to enter the Chinese market was making progress and discussion would focus chiefly on this subject. He had invited Charles

Deschamps, the head of the international division, to brief directors on the state of play in China. LFE was selling its goods in Europe, the US, Canada, Mexico and North Africa. The chairman had announced, almost a year earlier, that China might be an attractive market for LFE and the board had encouraged him to do some research and present an action plan.

Charles Deschamps gave his presentation with the aid of a deck of slides. His brief started with an estimate of the potential size of the Chinese market for the company's goods and an overview of potential competitors, mainly other European and US manufacturers. Charles Deschamps believed that, in China, there was a deep – and growing – market for high-quality, somewhat 'designer' food products imported from Europe. Chinese manufacturers were unlikely to offer much competition in the short term. The directors listened carefully. The market research had been done by a consultancy firm with a solid foothold in China.

Next, Mathieu Pomper, the chairman, added supporting comments to Charles Deschamps's presentation. Then he invited board members to ask questions. Only Carlo Davini, an independent director, raised points. He talked at length about the media coverage on the sharp correction in China's overvalued stock exchange, the depreciation of the yuan, the concerns being expressed in some media about a slowdown in the Chinese economy, the difficulties of operating in China, the risk that Chinese manufacturers would copy LFE's products and so on.

At this point the chairman politely interrupted and, on the grounds of time constraints, invited Deschamps to take the floor again. Deschamps continued his presentation about the plan to seek business in China. With the assistance of the same consultancy firm that had done the market research, LFE was forming a company in China and looking to recruit a country head. At first, LFE would make its entry into China through distributors, but the company was not ruling out a direct presence at selected points of sale (shopping 'golden miles', high-end shopping centres). As for the country head position, they were looking for a European or North American national – but preferably French – who already had some experience working in China and knew the language.

Marcel Laclede then interrupted to remind the board that he had formerly been a director of a leading French company that had had a presence in China since the 1990s. The way to open up the Chinese market, he said, was to find a local partner, locking down all the fine detail with the aid of a good law firm and agreeing on a partnership strategy. In his experience, he firmly asserted, the way to approach China was to go in with a partner.

Carla Ribaud, another independent director, had no experience with China, but had sat on the board of a company that had entered Latin America; this had been done directly, as LFE's head of the international division was proposing now and the venture had gone very well. She thought that going in with a partner might even complicate matters. Then she gently suggested: "It seems that Charles Deschamps has given this a lot of thought. Maybe we should let him finish."

Deschamps explained that the company was in the process of selecting two distributors on the basis of geographical presence. LFE had visited them in China, and the distributors had sent people to visit LFE's headquarters in France. There seemed to be a good relationship in the making. These were experienced distributors who were already working with other European and American clients – not competitors of LFE, but with a comparable standing. Deschamps also said that, through a well-known firm of headhunters with an office in China, the company was expecting to have two or three candidates to run the China venture within the coming month.

The independent director Marcel Laclede again insisted that the Chinese market was highly complex and it was almost impossible to find a European who was able to navigate it successfully. In his experience on that highly prestigious board of which he had formerly been a member, entry into difficult countries was always approached via a local partner and even then, success was not guaranteed. Carla Ribaud, however, congratulated Charles on his proposal. As a member of the appointments and remuneration committee, she offered to help him select the right candidate to run the Chinese operation and said that it would be a learning opportunity for her. The chairman thanked Carla for her offer and moved on to the next item on the agenda.

The Luxe Food Europe case study enacts two situations of the sort referred to earlier. First we have the 'chatterbox', Carlo Davini, speaking at length on topics that have been extensively covered by the media and are already known to the whole board; this is obviously a waste of time and the chairman was right to interrupt. Marcel Laclede, whom we might describe as a self-appointed 'expert', interrupts more than once, without fully stating his grounds, to propose an approach taken by a big company where he had formerly held a directorship for entering China.

Then we have a director, Carla Ribaud, who actually tries to support the work done by the head of the international division and the executive chairman by harnessing the board's ability to oversee key points – in this case, by involving the appointments and remuneration committee in selecting the China country head – while looking for ways to move forward.

DIRECTORS' ACCOUNTABILITY

If we were to count the number of directors right now who are in a position of statutory conflict of interest, we would come up with a figure in the tens of thousands and set to increase. While I was revising the manuscript for this book, the Volkswagen affair made headlines. This will be an historic milestone. Board accountability is comparable to other forms of professional accountability, such as in the world of medicine or government. It is only natural to expect people's activities to be subject to rules and those rules must be all the more demanding when the stakes are high. A doctor has human health – even human lives – in his or her hands. Directors, for their part, are responsible for the savings and jobs of thousands of people, and also for the interests of the company's customers.

Recently, I had the chance, in front of an audience of several hundred people, to introduce the Chinese magnate Ronnie Chan, the chairman and owner of a large corporate holding that encompasses businesses ranging from real estate firms in China to tech companies listed on the New York Stock Exchange.

Many years previously, I had met him discreetly in Hong Kong, when the media seemed to have his photograph on every page. He was the target of an enquiry relating to his membership of the board of Enron, which had just gone bankrupt in the midst of an obvious fraud. Finally, the justice system cleared his name: Enron had formed a board of world-class directors, but had kept them in the dark. The group's board was entirely disconnected from reality, despite being properly structured on the face of it.

At the presentation, Ronnie authorized me to explain all this. Jeffrey Sonnenfeld, the dean of the Yale School of Management, said of Enron that: "No corporation could have had more appropriate financial competencies and experience on its board."[8] Knowing Ronnie Chan, I am sure his decision to sit on the Enron board was not driven by the money or the prestige; he already had plenty of both. His motivation must have been a desire to learn, and improve, the governance of an ambitious international business project.

Very few directors engage in a rigorous legal scrutiny of the board they are joining. However, it is increasingly common for companies them-

"And, while there's no reason yet to panic, I think it only prudent that we make preparations to panic."

selves to offer coverage for the contingency of directors facing prosecution, litigation, or penalties, if appropriate, because shareholders cannot be expected to pay a fine on behalf of a dishonest director.

As mentioned earlier, one of the factors that makes this worse is that business is becoming subject to increasing regulation, but not in a uniform way globally. Transactions may be legal in some countries but illegal in others.

Other transactions may be on the legal borderline and can hurt shareholders, suppliers, or competitors, or those affected may use the possibility of legal action as a bargaining chip or as a way of covering up their own mistakes and transgressions. Many legal battles do not, in the end, lead to any penalty for the defendant company, but nonetheless grab media headlines and damage the reputation of the firm and the board. At the time of writing this book, the media was concerned with the $14.4 million fine paid by UBS in January 2015, while the New York attorney general was pressing charges against Barclays, and the Hong Kong government assessing a fine on BNP Paribas. The press had also been reporting that Volkswagen would have to spend very large amounts of money in recompense for cheating on its diesel engine emissions tests.

Most of these scandals revolve around irregularities committed in the context of placing financial products with investors. Other cases might simply have to do with maintaining or improving sales figures. Obviously, these penalties and the extensive media coverage are terrible publicity and no doubt they have prompted emergency board meetings, management firings and reshuffles, and board resignations. This is not something a director would put on his resumé.

CAJA DE AHORROS REGIONAL (CAR)

In late 2007, the board of Caja de Ahorros Regional, a typical Spanish savings bank, held a meeting. As usual, the board met at 1pm and continued, through lunch, from 2.30pm to 4pm. No information was supplied prior to the meeting nor circulated in the boardroom. Some of the figures were shown on screen and some were read out. The figures disclosed seemed fine to the directors. The savings bank was growing slightly faster than the wider economy and profitability was slightly above the banking industry average. The figure for non-performing loans and write-offs was very low. The savings bank operated a charitable foundation that supported a small regional university and awarded scholarships and bursaries for overseas study.

The bank did not supply detailed information about its lending. The figures were not itemized by borrower category or by purpose (mortgages, business loans, sales financing, consumer loans and so on). The reason for this was that if the bank had, for example, disclosed to the board the details of car sales financing for some of the stronger dealerships, other dealerships would have put pressure on the bank. The same might have happened with mortgage loans.

The board comprised 18 directors, the majority of whom were independent: people with strong reputations in the bank's savings section and former local government officials (regional government, the mayor of the region's capital, the principal of the region's public university). Two of the directors were the former chairman and CEO of the bank; they had left their positions on reaching retirement age.

José had been appointed to a chair of economics at the local university on his return from the US, where he had been awarded a doctorate and had taught for two years as a professor at one of the country's leading schools. In late 2007, he was invited to sit on the board of CAR. José seized the opportunity. His status as a chair professor placed him on the same footing as the rest of directors. The value of his academic training was beyond question. Moreover, the job wasn't very taxing in terms of time. He would be making good contacts and the remuneration package was attractive. After five years of living in America on a tight budget and having recently married, relocated, and bought a car and a house, the extra money would come in handy. He read a book or two about corporate governance and company boards.

At his first board meeting, José was introduced to the other attendees by the chairman, who then moved on to the items of the agenda. He read out some data on the savings bank's position and stressed that the figures were strong. He said the economy was doing well and there was a high demand for credit. José got the impression that the savings bank was doing brisk business in mortgage loans: in the area with the highest density of CAR branches, housing was being built at a swift rate and when he himself had applied for a mortgage, he had found himself stuck in a long queue. He asked whether he had guessed correctly, but the chairman replied that confidentiality prevented him from disclosing the bank's biggest-selling products. The directors should rest assured all the same, he said, that the loans granted had been carefully considered and were secured on adequate collateral.

The board was told that the bank had bought a stake in an innovative investment fund where other saving banks were also putting their money. The fund was betting that certain currencies, like the dollar, were overvalued and likely to depreciate. None of the directors reacted to this.

The chairman announced that, owing to the bank's strong performance in 2007, the management team would be rewarded with bonuses. In addition, their pay and pension benefits would be improved. He gave no specific figures. He did, however, specify the pay increase that would be awarded to board members. Discussion then turned to the recent changes in the management of another savings bank with which CAR had regular dealings – mention being made of the political background and possible changes on the board. There followed a wider conversation about the main political, economic, and business stories that were featuring in the media.

José wasn't expecting this. He didn't know what the bank was investing in, but he suspected it was mostly real estate business. He had read an article in a recent email newsletter from the US business school of which he was an alumnus, about the cyclical nature of the real estate sector. One of the leading professors at the business school had written the article, warning that a downturn was due soon – it was already beginning to be felt in the US, but would ultimately have global effects. The dollar, on the other hand, was set to rise, and the banking industry was in a parlous state owing to the overconfident investment spree in which it had engaged during the boom years.

Realizing that the chairman seemed perfectly content and unconcerned by any of these issues, José decided to contact his older sister, a lawyer at a prestigious practice. The siblings often shared their doubts and worries in a professional and confidential way. She told him that very few banks were following the rules on mortgage lending and credit to construction firms and developers strictly. Many of her clients, she said, had easily secured bank financing for projects that had been barely sketched out. She advised her brother to leave the board of CAR. "There's no way this can end well," she said. José followed her advice and resigned immediately, on the pretext that, for professional reasons, he was about to move to another city.

CAR was one of the banks that was hit hard by the financial crisis that struck Spain in 2009 and deepened even further in the following years. Several big deals, which had been entered into without proper controls, attracted media coverage and depositors who had been hurt levelled accusations at the bank's executives and directors for their carelessness – perhaps even bad faith.

We have seen that José was able to weigh the pros and cons of board membership from the standpoint of legal risk. He sought a legally qualified opinion on the situation and finally decided that, given these circumstances, there were more cons than pros. But there were 18 directors on the board, and the others seemed quite comfortable there, whether through ignorance, misplaced trust, or an overestimatation of their own abilities.

The board of directors is not a public relations outfit designed to project an image of seriousness, trustworthiness, and high calibre. Sometimes, senior executives and major shareholders think of the media impact of the board as its main purpose, a kind of assurance or endorsement. But some of the directors who are happy to belong to that select clique may be unaware of the risk that they are being played for fools.

On some boards, there is a rule in place that the secretary must report on any litigation in progress and on any issues that might eventually have legal repercussions, at each meeting. But sometimes it is the audit committee that focuses on these matters.

PROMOTORA LATINA GLOBAL (PLA)

Roger Lamb was remanded in custody on charges of having bribed senior government officials and corporate executives in Latin America. Promotora Latinoamericana Global was a company with a broad global reach, particularly in Latin America, where it had started to operate in the real estate development and construction business (blocks of flats, offices, shopping centres, roads, motorways, airports, and other infrastructure). Roger was the company's CEO and board chairman. When he was put behind bars, he didn't know what had happened to the other directors – he had been unable to talk to his lawyer. Everything had been a surprise. The first he knew of it was when the police came to his office with an arrest warrant signed by a judge and took him off to prison.

A few days later, now with the assistance of a top law firm, he learned that a manager in the finance and control department had been fired on suspicion of embezzlement. That person had then gone to the police with a detailed report of cash bribes that had been given to senior officials with key decision-making powers over the award of construction contracts, permits, changes to awarded projects, budget increases and so forth.

Most of these bribes had been small backhanders, but a few had been very substantial and the issue had been talked about at board meetings, albeit not in detail. The company had cash funds tied to the issuance of false invoices. The position of the management, and of the board, had always been that this was the only way to operate effectively in some markets. Their policy was to try to negotiate in such a way as to avoid having to bribe anyone and, most of all, to prevent company managers from benefiting themeselves. The board viewed these practices as a sort of 'disease' with which they simply had to live.

PLA executives knew that other firms also paid bribes, because the recipients and their associates had let them know. PLA's own lawyer did what he could to structure these irregular deals in the best way possible to avoid detection in the event of an enquiry.

Roger felt that the situation was unfair. The matter had become a media scandal which, according to Roger's lawyer, the head of the communications department was trying to contain. The media were pointing the finger at him as a criminal who was getting rich through fraudulent practices. Following his lawyer's instructions, Roger resigned from the chairmanship and from the board. The board appointed a new chairman from outside the company, with a strong track record and industry knowledge. No doubt the competition would grasp the opportunity to poach some of the projects on which PLA had been working hard.

Roger's lawyer had told him that he would probably be released from prison soon on the security of a bail bond. Later they would consider whether it was best to speed up proceedings and settle the matter by paying a fine or – if a prison sentence were in the cards – to try to delay the process for as long as possible.

What can we learn from Roger's experience? It's quite simple: you have to do the right thing. There are two very powerful reasons. First, it is our duty to behave ethically in all walks of life, including business. Second, there's no such thing as confidentiality and any misdemeanour will eventually come to light. In the information age, something that has been purportedly treated in confidence might be found, 30 minutes later, on social media, generating comments and debate.

The board of directors must use all available means (audit committee, statutory auditor, attendance at board meetings by senior executives, detailed analysis of major transactions) to ensure that everything the company does is strictly within legal bounds.

Of course, some markets are more corrupt than others. But it's also true that some companies give up on certain markets precisely because it is so difficult to do anything legally. And some companies are able to operate in those markets without breaking the law, by virtue of one or more of the following factors: sheer brand power; social contributions that are known to and valued by, key figures in the community, such that the company's reputation for ethics becomes a force of attraction in itself; or standards of technology and competitiveness that set the company apart from the competition.

BOARD
REMUNERATION

Every company, and every country, is different. But we are now seeing increasing convergence across the world. Companies are extending their reach to the global scale, and boards of directors are acquiring an international perspective by appointing people of different nationalities and with international track records. We can expect that, by 2020, remuneration will find its own level internationally.

Everywhere in the world, the key variable determining board remuneration is the size of the company. A number of consultancy firms have produced research on board remuneration and of course, the figures provided in the research are just broad averages for directors at companies of varying sizes. But this information is valuable, insofar as it can reassure directors that their remuneration is in line with that paid by the company's peers. It is unusual for a company to disclose directors' remuneration individually (outside studies preserve confidentiality), but they do sometimes publish the total remuneration due to the board as a whole, thus providing a fairly clear guide to what an individual director can expect to be paid.

Board remuneration comprises several components. Some companies pay a fixed sum only, while others introduce a variable element. The fixed pay may break down into basic pay, attendance per diems, and remuneration for committee membership (members of the audit, appointments and remuneration, and strategy committees). Variable pay may take the form of a bonus tied to the achievement of targets; part of the bonus may be paid in company shares. At some unlisted companies, these shares belong to a fund set up for the specific purpose of remunerating directors and senior executives. The value of the fund is determined in parallel with the value of the company, in accordance with a given formula. If the company puts in an outstanding performance, its value is likely to rise and the value of the fund would then rise too. Subject to various conditions (length of service with the company after receiving the 'shares'), executives can convert the shares to cash within the same fund.

"Tell the public we don't want to hurt anyone. All we want is their money."

Many companies have kept their directors' remuneration unchanged throughout the years of the economic downturn, but from 2014 onwards remuneration is rising and the lost ground is likely to be made up in the coming years.

Some highly tentative figures have been provided, based on a range of recent research papers. A director at a company with revenue of less than €500 million a year could be making about €60,000 per annum, not counting remuneration for committee membership, which could come to about €12,000 per committee. At companies making revenue of €1 billion to €2 billion, those figures would increase to €80,000 and €15,000, respectively. At companies making revenue of €10 billion or more, those figures would increase to about €150,000 and €20,000, respectively. Of course, some directors are paid far more than this. These figures include variable pay. If the director needs to travel, air fares, hotel and other expenses would be covered separately.

At most companies, nonexecutive directors are paid the same. Executive directors, on the other hand, may have their salaries as executives raised to reflect their additional dedication and duties as directors.

If a company is listed and part of variable pay takes the form of shares, the amount is valued at the price prevailing at the time of payment. If the company is not listed, a notional company value can be assessed using a specific formula (for instance, 10 x Earnings Before Interest, Taxes, Depreciation and Amortisation (EBITDA), minus debt). Senior executives and directors may be paid in shares that can be converted into cash only after a certain lapse of time. This is intended to stimulate long-term value creation and to retain those executives and directors.

DEUTSCHE UNIVERSALE MECHANISMEN (DUM)

Hellmut Burgelmann joined the board of DUM as an independent director in 2014, with remuneration of €80,000. In January 2015, one year after his appointment, the chairman told Hellmut that, since 2014 had been a good year and DUM was happy with his contribution, his pay in 2015 would amount to €90,000. He also suggested that Hellmut join the audit committee to replace a director who had been on it for the past three years (DUM's policy was to rotate committee members every three years). The additional remuneration would be €25,000.

The DUM board met ten times a year, at the end of every month except July and December. Each meeting lasted a whole working day (from 9am to 5pm). There were ten board members, three of whom were company executives – including the CEO (who was also the board chairman) – three were shareholder appointees (the company was listed) and three were independents. The audit committee held three-hour meetings four times a year, on the afternoon of the day preceding a board meeting.

Hellmut was also on the boards of a prestigious car manufacturer and a major chemical producing company. He had spent most of his career at a leading consultancy firm, and his directorship positions were offered to him by the companies with whom he had worked as a consultant. DUM engaged in the manufacture of highly specialized machines for packaging pharmaceuticals, certain food products, and consumer goods such as creams and fragrances. It also made devices for production chain automation.

While travelling to a DUM board meeting, in the business lounge of the Munich airport, Hellmut bumped into an old friend, Mark, who was on the return leg from Shanghai, where he had attended a machinery trade fair. Mark told him that, at the fair, he had spoken to the chairman and chief technology and operations officer of DUM, both of whom he knew well. The fair had been very interesting, Mark said and DUM had been an exhibitor. Mark was unaware that Hellmut was on the DUM board. Mark mentioned that, a year ago, the chairman had offered him a place on the board as an independent director. Mark was unable to accept at the time because he then held – and still did, hence his attendance at the Shanghai fair – a directorship at a company whose business partly overlapped with DUM's. The DUM chairman had offered Mark €150,000 for the directorship and a further €25,000 for sitting on the audit committee.

Hellmut knew Mark well and valued him highly. But he felt immensely frustrated to learn that Mark had been offered almost twice as much pay as Helmut for performing the same duties. Helmut had assumed that all the independent directors and shareholder appointees received equal pay. He felt somewhat unsettled and had no clear idea what to do.

Turning the matter over in his mind, he realized that the chairman's offer to Mark may have hinged on the fact that Mark was already on the board of a similar firm, and would bring with him both relevant industry expertise and a wealth of knowledge about the competing company, thus helping DUM in its plans for growth, diversification, and potential takeovers. In Helmut's case, however, joining the DUM board had involved a period of training and he could not, at first, contribute as much value as Mark would have done. Even so, the difference still seemed very stark to him and the recent pay raise now appeared trifling in the light of what had been offered to Mark. It was a further unpleasant surprise that, despite Hellmut's obvious willingness to learn, he had not been invited to the Shanghai trade fair.

Hellmut resolved to talk openly to the chairman about his misgivings. He framed his query not as a complaint but as a request for guidance on how to improve in his role. He rated Mark very highly and understood perfectly well that Mark's contribution would have been greater than his own.

The chairman thanked Hellmut for his openness and explained that he had approached Mark at the suggestion of a headhunter, who also proposed the remuneration figure. At the time, the DUM board was considering a takeover and, moreover, one of the most experienced directors had to retire owing to ill health. The takeover had finally fallen through, because a US firm looking to gain a foothold in Europe had moved in faster and paid what the chairman believed to be an inflated price. The average remuneration paid to DUM directors was below the figure offered to Mark, but the aim was to increase that average gradually, over time. The consultancy firm had examined the matter and the executive directors had followed their conclusions.

The chairman apologized for the fact that remuneration had not been discussed openly by the full board. The fact was that it remained a highly sensitive issue because each of the directors had joined at a different time and under different circumstances, so not everyone was being paid the same. The chairman said he was aware he needed to address this point head-on and promised to bring it up at a board meeting in the near future. As to the Shanghai fair, he again apologized and said that he thought it would have been too much to ask Hellmut to devote the several days required to attend. He thanked Hellmut for his interest in learning and promised to bear it in mind on future occasions.

Clearly, if instead of speaking out modestly, respectfully, and openly to the chairman, Helmut had kept the matter to himself and allowed his frustration to stew, things would have been a lot worse. By speaking up, he probably helped to speed up the process of board professionalization and director training and to bring remuneration into alignment with the standard for companies like DUM. What's more, if cronyism really was putting board remuneration out of balance, Helmut had given the chairman a timely reminder that there's no such thing as confidentiality.

This case study also features an appropriate response on the part of the chairman. He plainly values Hellmut and accordingly apologizes and promises more openness and professionalism in the future.

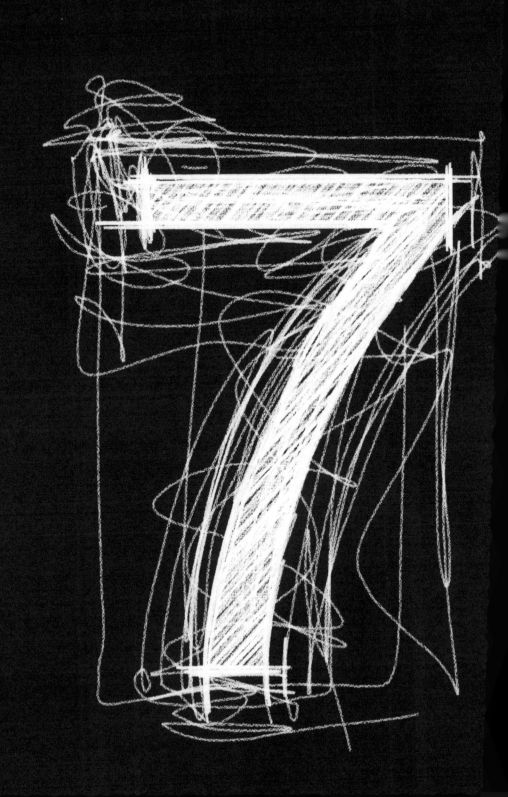

BOARD
ASSESSMENT

Even now, there are still many company boards that do not undergo any rigorous assessment of their performance. Assessment models exist, however and this is a practice that some legal services and consultancy firms have thoroughly mastered. The method described below arises from research conducted into certain assessment processes and from other available information related to this.

The first question might be: who should conduct the assessment? Sometimes an independent director's experience makes him or her well-suited to the job. Sometimes, the assessment role is taken up by a board committee, either the audit committee or a committee established especially for the purpose. And sometimes, assessment is commissioned from a firm of consultants with an established practice in this field.

The method of assessment generally involves an analysis of usual practices based on information obtained from the board secretary and chairman and subsequent interviews with board members. The assessment result is usually submitted to the board for discussion and the board's conclusions serve as the final touch.

The following points are assessed:

a) Board format: number of directors; frequency and duration of meetings

b) Board members: director categories (proprietary, executive, independent); directors' training and experience; international directors; women on the board

c) Information supplied to the board: regular reporting (annual accounts, accounts itemized by business unit); specific information on individual issues addressed in board discussions; information on the industry and competitors; information on the monitoring of especially significant issues (legal matters, negotiations with unions, restructuring processes)

d) Board discipline: directors' attendance record; commitment (preparation, contribution of relevant information on topics that may affect or be of interest to the company); participation in board discussions

e) Board management: appropriate time and agenda management; appropriate drafting of board minutes; quality of the information supplied and timeliness of supply in advance of board meeting dates

f) Board proceedings: chairman's and secretary's ability to encourage and guide a climate of open discussion, leading to constructive and progressive debate, enabling the involvement of those directors who would otherwise be less able to contribute to the conversation and handling those who obstruct progress by unwittingly repeating themselves

g) Board meetings outside the boardroom: board meetings held at company production facilities, overseas offices, or during international industry fairs and events. Such actions may prove a powerful aid to directors' understanding of the company and its position in the industry

h) Involvement of executives in board meetings: to enhance the board's discussion of certain topics by inviting company executives to attend, thus enabling directors to get to know the management

i) The board and the CEO: although the CEO is a board member, assessment must turn to the question of the extent to

"*Ask the judge whether we can find the defendant not guilty and still execute him.*"

which he or she listens to the board and is accountable to it for implementing its decisions

j) Value creation by the board: in connection with the previous point, the actions encouraged or adopted by the board, and executed by the CEO, should give the board a sense that real value is being created for shareholders and that the company's long-term interests are being properly served

k) Legal matters: it is important to evaluate the extent to which the board is aware of the laws and regulations applicable to the business and to ensure that 'compliance' and 'legal risk' criteria are applied to all significant decisions

l) Board remuneration: since broad guidelines are available on board remuneration, based on company size and even company type, it may be appropriate for this aspect to be assessed as well. If directorships are highly demanding but insufficiently paid, this may lead to a loss of talent

These are also valid points for an assessment of board committees. For a board of directors to function properly, it is important that its committees – which are subsets of the board – perform to an appropriate standard in relation to the points listed above.

ASSESSMENT OF THE CEO

At some company boards, assessment of the board as a whole is linked to a specific assessment of the CEO, who is often also the board chairman. The following points are usually considered when assessing the performance of the CEO:

a) Qualifications. Having earned an MBA at a world-class business school is not the same as having started one's career without any sort of university qualification, even if this was not a choice but a necessity. Regardless of previous experience and education, qualifications and training can be updated at any time, and career businesspeople need to find the time to pursue this on an ongoing basis. Those who took their MBA at leading business schools 20 years ago did little work, for instance, on the digital world or on global management in emerging economies like India, China, Africa, or Russia and did not develop sufficient familiarity with the complexity and rich possibilities of the capital markets. A career businessperson is called on to master all these subject areas if he or she aims to be leading a company in 2020.

b) Leadership. The CEO must be able to set a clear goal for the company and motivate the team to follow him or her in that direction. The CEO's leadership must fire up the team's enthusiasm and encourage members to make suggestions and take the initiative. In an environment in which business moves quickly, opportunities must be identified and swiftly transformed into entrepreneurial action. Opportunities become visible to many different people. When people are encouraged to see them, when they feel listened to and supported in putting them into practice, that's entrepreneurial leadership.

c) Balance of dedication to strategy and operations. Both themes are important. A CEO who only thinks about strategy can bring the business to halt, while one who obsesses about operational details may be wasting everyone's time. It is vital to find the right balance between addressing each of these areas of concern, encouraging their organizational improvement and implementation. When the CEO's performance is assessed, the presence or absence of the right balance is clearly visible to the management team.

d) Information to the board and shareholders. The CEO must ensure that there is an appropriate flow of information to the board and shareholders. The information must be relevant, complete and up to date. In a world in which there's no such thing as confidentiality, it is important to make sure that information flows to lower levels in the organization. If this is done properly, the whole team will be motivated and enthusiastic.

e) Feedback. The management team expects the CEO to supply feedback on its performance. Suitable feedback is a stimulus for enhanced management, training, and implementation of the management's ideas and values.

f) Executives' sense of trust and belonging. If the above conditions are satisfied, executives feel comfortable working for the CEO. The fast pace of the modern business world, and the uncertainty generated by technological progress do, of course, create a measure of stress. But that stress is shared by the entire team.

g) Ethics. Ethical values are acquiring increasing importance in the corporate world. There continue to exist large regions with severe shortfalls in terms of ethical business conduct, such as Latin America, Africa, parts of Asia, Russia and so on. But it is important to spread, throughout the organization, a rock-solid conviction that every decision must be ethical. Negotiations may become more protracted and tougher, but in the final analysis, ethics must always win through. Many companies have achieved this. It's not an impossibility. What's more, business ethics is a very broad-ranging area that faces internal challenges, such as discrimination and favouritism.

GLOBAL PRINTING SERVICES (GPS)

Jay Lewis was the CEO of Global Printing Service (GPS) and also chairman of the board. The board had determined that an assessment of its own performance should be conducted every three years by a specialized firm of consultants. Jay had just received the assessment report issued by the consultancy firm. The consultants had interviewed the members of the board and key people on the management team who sat on the executive committee. In addition, the assessors had compared the data with the information available on analogous companies. GPS was a global distributor of printing materials and equipment (for industrial, office, and personal use).

The assessment report highlighted the following points: there were too many directors (16, whereas the average for similar companies was 12); all the directors were US nationals and lacked meaningful international experience; board remuneration was 25% below the average for industry peers – and, in fact, over the past two years, two directors had left, no doubt because they had received better offers elsewhere. All the directors had been assessed positively except for two – one spent too much time talking about irrelevant matters, while another was untrained in finance and tended to obstruct discussions with unhelpful questions and comments.

The report contained a range of recommendations addressed to the chairman himself. He should make board debates more productive through suitable time management and monitoring of time spent, improved presentation and timeliness of information supplied to directors (at least one week in advance of each meeting; at some GPS board meetings, the data was supplied only in the boardroom itself) and increased presence, on a rotating basis, of GPS executives at board meetings, to enrich directors' understanding of the business.

Jay was unsure how to react. Having thought about the implications of the report and talked to the consultants, he came to the conclusion that it was pointless commissioning a board assessment if the recommended corrections and improvements were not implemented.

He spoke in private to the two directors who had been negatively assessed. In both cases, the directors offered to resign. Jay accepted their resignations. He wondered whether to ask one of the two to stay on for a period, but remembered that there's no such thing as confidentiality and decided to let them both go at once, leaving the rest of the board to come up with their own theories as to why. He decided not to replace them and paid them the remuneration that would have been due for a half-year period, which was a pleasant surprise for them.

Next, he decided to increase board remuneration by 25%. Two of the directors had been on the board for ten years and, under the new rules suggested by the consultants, this meant they had exhausted their terms. In one of the two cases, Jay was happy to let the director go. But the other director was often a great help and Jay wanted to retain him. He spoke to the consultants. They proposed that he should follow the time-limit rule, but engage the outgoing director under a one-year consultancy contract, with the special aim of helping Jay to improve his management of the board. Jay was pleased with the idea and put it into practice.

The GPS case study shows how board assessment may lead to improved board performance. The reality is that the effectiveness of a board shows through only in the medium and long term, but Jay's willingness to make changes sends a signal to directors that improvement is the goal. The increased remuneration is also likely to be a powerful stimulus. The fact that Jay himself is willing to receive advice, monitoring, and training from an outgoing director, who is probably highly rated by his former colleagues, would also appear to be a positive and encouraging step.

Perhaps Jay could have asked the consultants to give a presentation based on a slimmed-down version of their report. Any form of assessment is an exam of sorts, and those assessed await their 'grade' or 'mark' with a degree of trepidation. This means the process needs to be fairly swift, from announcing the assessment and implementing it through to taking key decisions in light of the results.

OTHER TYPES OF BOARDS

The concept of corporate governance can be extended to other key activities within the company, such as those carried out by board committees. Moreover, some companies create advisory boards that are separate from the board of directors, although some members of the advisory board may also be directors. Advisory boards may oversee activities in a given country that is of special importance to the company, or address the company's concerns in a particular area, such as technology. Internal rules are made to specify these boards' degree of responsibility and their internal functioning (meetings, venue, remuneration and so on).

The institution of an 'advisory board' or 'advisory council' extends the concept of corporate governance beyond the business world to the academic, social, and political domains. It is common in academic administration to set up an 'international advisory board' comprising leading academics, businesspeople, and professionals who guide and oversee the institution's affairs. Some government bodies also create advisory boards in support of economic and social initiatives in a given city or region. The practice is widespread in family-business associations, industry associations, and professional associations in the fields of architecture, medicine and law.

The underlying principles of boards of directors in the world of business apply also to advisory boards in other spheres although, of course, specific rules must be made to ensure that they function efficiently and effectively in their own remit. Ethical failures in nonbusiness boards can be as harmful as in their corporate counterparts – for instance, if the members of an advisory board were to benefit improperly from an association's funds.

A field in which boards are playing an increasingly significant role is nonprofit entities. Professors Marc Epstein (Rice University) and Warren McFarlan (Harvard Business School)[9] have specifically researched this area. They conclude that corporate governance, as discussed so

SIPRESS

"I'd like to take a moment to define what I mean by 'defining moment.'"

far in this book, is just as useful and necessary, if not more so, in the nonprofit arena.

As explained in chapter 2, there is a trend toward the creation of 'disruptive councils'. These are a form of advisory board whose discussions are separate from the organization's specific strategies and circumstances and broadly cover the themes of social, economic, technological, and political change. The disruptive council will aim to identify factors that might eventually affect the entity or offer attractive opportunities for diversification.

For instance, one disruptive council scrutinized case studies of conventional companies that had bought start-ups at exceptionally high prices. Public information confirmed that a number of conventional firms – pharmaceuticals, materials, distribution and so on – had bought start-ups at prices that far exceeded the value that would have been determined under ordinary financial criteria. The ensuing analysis revealed that these moves reflected the aim to access potential that perhaps ought to have been targeted by investment in research and development, in high-potential emerging regions, or areas in which competitors were increasing their capabilities.

Frequently, a leap of this sort is not readily perceived to make sense by a conventional board whose expectations assume the company's continuity in its existing business areas and markets.

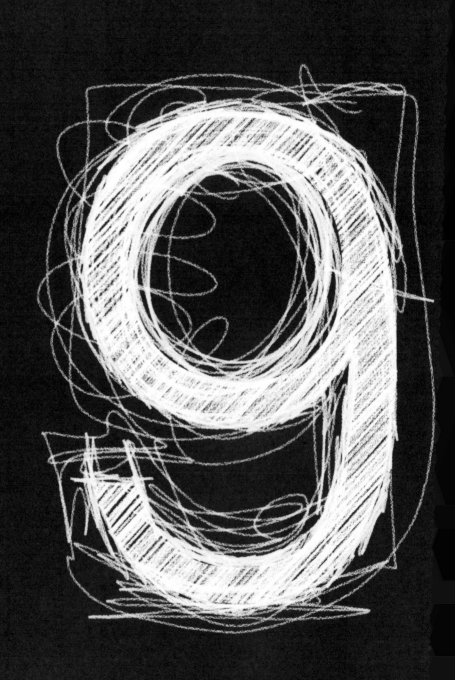

WHAT
ABOUT SMALL
COMPANIES?

The concept of a board of directors is usually associated with large or medium-sized companies. Many companies with years of history behind them and those headed by an entrepreneur – or even by the original entrepreneur's successor – have not even considered establishing a board of directors. Around the world, you can still find entrepreneurs who believe company boards are pointless, or even detrimental to growth; the board is viewed as expensive and entirely dispensable. Perceptions of this kind are more widespread among small and medium-sized enterprises.

Yet many start-ups formed under the wing of venture capital firms or business angels set up a board immediately. The board generally comprises shareholders or their appointees, but may also include independent directors. Good corporate governance is a requirement imposed by the investors who pay the start-up's bills.

So there remains a large number of companies of all sizes – but smaller firms especially – where corporate governance is still not regarded as particularly helpful. Nevertheless, corporate governance continues to move centre-stage and it is likely that, by 2020, we will see rapid growth in the number of small and medium-sized companies overseen by boards of directors.

The trend seen in small and medium-sized firms is to set up a fairly small board of directors comprising one or two independent members, the owners (who are often involved in managing the business) and one or two senior executives. These mini-boards, which are often not formally constituted under the law, try to follow the principles of good corporate governance. This approach can be a positive start. Moreover, an independent director's dispassionate outside view can be useful in dispelling small business owners' self-deception as to their company's future, which they have not examined in sufficient detail: all too often, they have no future at all. Many of the small and medium-sized enterprises that collapsed during the recent economic downturn could have been sold at an excellent price in the first half of the 2000s.

*"If there's no more old business and no more
new business, let's declare bankruptcy."*

If, after having analyzed a small business, a consultant feels that its future is unpromising but that it might be profitably sold to a larger firm wanting to gain a foothold in the given country or sector, the entrepreneurs' typical response is, "But what would I do after that?" Being head of the company has become a pleasant routine keeping them busy and earning them kudos.

The "what would I do afterwards?" mindset is a recipe for self-deception. But if the idea of selling the business emerges in the course of a board discussion, it is less likely to be defeated.

The spread of the 'business angel' concept may be one antidote to the "what would I do afterwards?" attitude. We are beginning to see people who have become far more successful during the 'afterwards' period than they ever were as entrepreneurs in small businesses with no real future.

CARES

The acronym CARES stands for Car E-Sales: online car sales. The founders were alumni of an MBA programme at a leading business school. They set up a website as a platform for selling used cars. The internet was full of offers to sell used cars, from used car dealers, manufacturer dealerships, and private sellers. The most common selling process was a form of online auction, where the highest bidder would win the car.

The novelty introduced by CARES was to supply a 'certificate' for the car being put up for sale. The start-up formed a network of car experts, mostly skilled mechanics and engineers who had retired from car manufacturing companies and dealerships. A person wishing to sell his or her car would supply their physical address to CARES and the company would send the nearest expert to look at the car and issue a rating based on a predetermined set of indicators (state of the bodywork, state of the interior, engine functioning, tyres and so on). The overall rating would take the form of 'superior', 'average', or 'inferior'. The certification details were attached to the overall rating as a supporting document. The 'certifiers' were paid in the form of a commission on the sale price. The plan was to hold an annual event with their 'certifiers' to find ways of improving the process and invite guest speakers whose reputations would add value to the fact of holding 'CARES certifier' status.

The venture started to take off. The two entrepreneurs who had launched the start-up three years after completing their MBAs had spent their evenings and weekends designing the project and put their savings into setting it in motion. The project seemed to be going well and the founders believed it had immense potential. However, the concept was easy to copy and there was a high risk that an established industry player – such as a dealership or a spare parts distributor – would copy it. This drove them to seek rapid growth that would garner them the lion's share of the potential market.

In order to achieve rapid growth, they had to improve website functionality continuously, secure a strong selection of 'certifiers' and provide them with suitable training, constantly raising awareness of the service among people wishing to sell their cars and obtaining ongoing feedback on the entire process (satisfaction among buyers, sellers, and certifiers, market availability of alternative services, and additional services such as repairs and financing). All this required financing, which they had to find on the market.

The two entrepreneurs behind CARES were joint CEOs, one of whom focused mainly on the website, while the other was chiefly concerned with certifiers (selection, training, and follow-up). They had three employees: two supporting the website CEO, and the third acting as assistant to the certifier CEO. Throughout 2014, they held several meetings with venture capital firms. They had estimated they needed about €2 million to ensure self-sustaining accelerated growth – which, they had decided, should be international in scope.

In late 2014, through a network of business angels, they found three investors who were willing to put up the cash (€1 million up front, and €1 million six months later, in accordance with their forecast cash needs). But the three business angels wanted to follow the project closely through a board of directors. After discussing the details of this, it was agreed to form a board of directors comprising the two entrepreneurs – who would take turns to chair the board – the three investors, and a reputable car industry expert with an interest in start-ups.

For at least the first two years, neither the entrepreneurs nor the investors would be paid for their directorships. The independent director would be paid a very modest fee, to be increased two years later. In 2015 things got off to a good start and both the entrepreneurs and the other directors were happy with how things were going.

Over the past 15 years, the phenomenon of entrepreneurship has gained currency at breakneck speed around the world. A new business is often a source both of innovation and jobs and safeguards the continuity of a society largely based on the value created by private enterprise. This fact has been clearly understood by governments, universities, capital markets, companies, the professions, and the wider community.

Projects fostering the creation of new enterprises, with the support of universities, governments, chambers of commerce, banks, and other players follow professionally designed models. Those models embrace the idea of endowing each start-up with a company board. Entrepreneurs' natural enthusiasm needs to be tempered by a rigorous outside perspective that can be supplied by an experienced independent professional.

There is an increasing number of people with significant savings who choose to put their money into a project to which they can contribute ideas and experience and on which they can make a considerable return. Members of this new class of investors are termed 'business angels', although some entrepreneurs might be tempted to call them 'business devils' because they defend their investments so fiercely.

The board of a start-up often comprises the entrepreneurs themselves, business angels, the appointee of a private equity firm or venture capital fund – if this source of financing has been resorted to – and an independent director. The independent director may have agreed to work unpaid, or for a modest fee, on the strength of the promise of a future reward in the form of a bonus or a percentage of the proceeds of sale or stock-market flotation.

The CARES entrepreneurs had the benefit of belonging to an eco-system in which entrepreneurial opportunities were highly valued, an attractive ecosystem in 2015. The three investors proposed several names for the independent directorship positions through the network of business angels to which they belonged and through the business school that formed the background to the whole venture. Their idea was to find someone who knew the car industry well and was in a position of settled affluence (having successfully sold a company or retired on favourable terms), whose intention was not to start up any new companies but to take up directorships and advise companies on an occasional basis. Their aim was to recruit someone who would command the three business angels' respect, given that the CARES founders wanted to keep them in check.

Finally, they found someone who had devoted his entire career to the car industry – first at component manufacturers and later at car manufacturers themselves – and who had, on three occasions, held senior positions in a global setting. Having retired at the age of 65, in 2015 this person was 71. He was on the boards of three well-known companies. In 2010, he had invested in a start-up and had recently sold his stake at a significant profit. He was willing to join the CARES board and to devote considerable time to the venture for an annual fee of €20,000. After negotiations, it was agreed that he would be entitled to variable remuneration if CARES succeeded. The entrepreneurs viewed him as the ideal candidate, and the investors were also happy with the appointment.

The example of CARES shows how good corporate governance can be applied even to a start-up that has not yet proved that it can even be a business and where the number of board members equals the employee headcount. All the directors are, of course, contributing significantly to the enterprise from their various perspectives (management, ownership, independent view). Each of them has much to gain from the success of the project. And at a time when emotions, stress, rapid change, and the risk of failure (both professional and financial) are all running high, it is important for there to be a member of a company board who is capable of observing the business from a different, dispassionate, realistic, and long-term perspective.

WHAT IS DISTINCTIVE ABOUT FAMILY BUSINESSES?

Many of the purposes that are typical of family businesses can also be achieved by means of a board of directors and everything we have seen so far in this book about corporate governance and company boards applies just as well to a family-owned company. Some special features should be highlighted, however. Amy Schuman, Stacy Stutz and John Ward have focused their research on the distinctive hallmarks of family businesses.[10] Miguel Ángel Gallo has undertaken an in-depth exploration of the boards of family-owned companies.[11]

One of the special features of this segment of business is that a family that owns a company seeks to exercise very tight control. They do, of course, have the power to appoint and remove directors. Sometimes the family creates a 'family council' that focuses on the family's specific concerns (family members' education, wealth management and representation in a wide variety of social domains). The family council is often in charge of appointing the members of the company board. If the family has several companies under its ownership, the family council is responsible for appointing all their directors.

Some families are comfortable with the idea of having an independent director on their family council who is able, among other things, to defuse any tension that might arise between family members.

One of the main hallmarks of family-owned companies is that they take the long-term view. Family members are usually concerned with passing on the business to the next generation. This obviously entails effective management and a properly designed and updated strategy. This long-term perspective differs markedly from the very short-term view sometimes taken by the board of a listed company, where directors might be worried about the price at which the share will be trading the following day. Listed companies are, of course, capable of heeding long-term concerns, but family-owned companies are highly distinctive in this respect.

"First of all, this meeting never happened."

Another trait of family businesses is that they often display a high degree of acceptance and tolerance of diversification, which their boards may positively encourage. Listed companies, however, tend toward a narrow focus, this being the approach preferred by the capital markets. Analysts' preferred technique for evaluating a listed company is to compare it with other companies that are as similar as possible. Comparing Ford with General Motors is obviously easier than comparing General Electric with Philips: the first pair of firms focus on cars, while the second pair encompass a wide range of business segments. What's more, diversification can be one way of protecting long-term interests: some businesses may become less attractive and can be dropped in an orderly way, while others can be beefed up. This would be the case with Philips, for example, which made an orderly retreat from the home appliances industry and bolstered its medical unit.

Family values may translate into corporate values. Some family businesses require family members who take up company duties to be highly qualified (graduate and postgraduate education at international institutions). If the family-owned business has an international reach, family members are generally required to become involved for a time with subsidiaries or overseas units. Perhaps the most distinctive feature is that remuneration at family-owned companies (even at board level) is more modest than at listed companies and non-family businesses. It is an accepted truth with them that the value created by the business is the future of the family and needs to be carefully protected: not a penny more than necessary should be spent. Paloma Fernández[12] and John Ward[13], among others, have explored these features of family-owned companies.

The need to protect accumulated value also means that a family council is likely to follow a highly conservative dividend policy. The question of dividends is apt to prompt a family debate on the purposes of the value created by the family's companies. Part of that value may be paid out in the form of dividends, part of it may remain within the company (thus endowing it with a robust balance sheet, to accommodate growth and acquisitions or, in the worst cases, restructuring) and part may be extracted from the company and put into a family fund managed by what is generally termed the 'family office'. The family fund is then invested, whether in stocks, real estate, venture capital, or other assets. See María Fernández-Moya and Rafael Castro-Balaguer in relation to this.[14]

Another common characteristic of family businesses is that family members take a great interest in obtaining information about the family's companies and their performance. The markets in general are, of course, very concerned about the success or otherwise of listed companies, but the very fact that a family's wealth is tied up in the specific companies that it owns and in the 'family office' means that, in the event of any shift in the economic environment, family members have a lot of questions about how this might affect their business. This may lead to the creation of a specific reporting function, which may have its seat in the 'family office' or may be implemented informally by the CEO (or the CEO and the chairman, if these positions are held by different people).

On one occasion, I invited the chairman of a fairly large multinational company to speak at a major conference. He had been hired to troubleshoot the difficulties into which the company had run. In the space of one year, he had made far-reaching changes and returned the company to an excellent state of health. Soon afterwards, I read in the news that the chairman had been fired for undisclosed reasons. I failed to resist the temptation to call him and ask what had happened. He blamed himself and said: "I didn't pay enough attention to the fact that, although the company was listed, it was mostly owned by the family. I was good at supplying information to market analysts, but didn't do enough to answer questions from family members about concerns that I did not believe were particularly urgent or important. Now I know what needs to be done when heading up a family-owned company. You have to devote a lot of time to the family." These words of his were, to me, a clear confirmation of what we have discussed above.

We might say, by way of summary, that corporate governance in a family-owned company requires a special sort of attention to detail in response to the concerns of the owners, who are committed to – almost trapped in – the business over the long term, even though the underlying principles remain the same. We have also highlighted that the family has the power to make and break the company board and to impose certain priorities and values that shape key aspects of the life of the company. This can be formalized as a 'family protocol' that provides an overarching framework for the board's role and corporate governance over the long term. Josep Tapies, the chair professor of family-owned business at IESE, has explored these distinctive characteristics in great depth.[15]

WHAT DIFFERENCES ARE TO BE FOUND AROUND THE WORLD?

We live in a global environment. Digitalization helps us to break through borders and frontiers. Business management expertise is valid everywhere in the world. Companies are extending their scope of action globally. Corporate governance, like other aspects of business management, should apply in the same way across the planet.

It is nonetheless clear that business environments can differ widely and those differences have an impact on the effectiveness of corporate governance. For instance, if we compare the US with Europe, we find that the US is a huge single market equipped with a clear and rigorous legal system that speeds up the pace of business and lends clarity to the legal screening of board decisions.

In Europe, on the other hand, we have a mosaic of countries, jurisdictions, standards of rigour and constant political shifts that affect the laws applicable to business. This set of circumstances detracts from the agility of the analysis and implementation of business decisions. And if we look at emerging economies – Latin America, China, India, Southeast Asia, or Africa – we find mosaics that are more complex still, a more severe lack of legal rules and, all too often, serious ethical shortfalls.

But a company's global deployment requires it to function effectively in all these different settings and the role of the board of directors is to ensure that deployment is swift and accurate, but also legal, ethical, and socially responsible. Let's remember, yet again, that in the digital world there is no such thing as confidentiality and businesses must move quickly and with the utmost honesty and transparency. The nature of international leadership is now a priority in the business world and is attracting increasingly close study. (See Jordi Canals, managing director of IESE.[16,17])

If we were to enter the boardroom of a leading company in China, Russia, Brazil, or South Africa today, we would be likely to find the

"We made a miscalculation, but it's consistent with our over-all strategy."

company's accounts audited by one of the Big Four firms; to discover that the CEO has an MBA from Harvard Business School; and that the company is advised by a highly reputable law firm. But if we were to cast our gaze over the company's history, we would begin to see things that are harder to understand. Many companies in emerging economies have created value in the real estate sector. Some are not adequately aware of this fact. This also happened in Europe and the US, but many years ago. In a context of doubtful legality, these ventures prospered with the aid of politicians and government officials. These countries' economic development paved the way for growth across all sectors. There were opportunities to operate as local partners for multinationals, to copy business models and to do business as a licensee or franchisee, all of which helped the rise of a stronger and more comprehensive economy.

Even today, it is not uncommon to see companies (including large ones) operate under a cloud of doubtful ethics and in 2015 we have witnessed government officials in developing countries going to prison for corruption. We know of companies that have simply given up on the notion of operating in certain regions and from time to time, a company makes a seemingly unexplained exit from an emerging market, despite its potential. The undisclosed reason is often connected with corporate governance: the board chooses to sacrifice the business over falling into the trap of unethical practices, because it knows there is no such thing as confidentiality.

In 2015, you can travel to a country in sub-Saharan Africa and see large office blocks occupied by US and European companies such as Nestlé, Unilever, or Coca Cola, or a Chinese company like Haier. You might walk past a Mercedes-Benz dealership, or read in the paper that China Development Bank will be financing the construction of a railway across Africa. Or you might go to China and find out that it is the world's third largest market for Coca-Cola, which plans to invest $5 billion there from 2015 to 2018. You will see the offices of the same

"We do it, Havermeyer, because our corporate parent says we must."

European companies, discover that Citibank has opened a large complex and walk past another Mercedes-Benz dealership. Behind these global deployments, which keep standards of quality high and act within the law, we find proactive governing bodies that are capable of stimulating the process, enlisting the support of consultancy firms and law partnerships, introducing incentives and new hires, and recruiting capable and locally experienced directors to local boards.

Looking forward to 2020, international deployment can only increase and acquire importance in the role of company boards. Digitalization may have a significant impact. E-commerce is growing faster in Africa and China than in some developed economies. We are unlikely to see as many bank branches in Africa as we still do in Europe and the US, where banks are looking at ways of closing down many of their physical branches. The dearth of bank branches has driven many Africans to interact with their banks by phone. This is obviously a step forward in online and mobile banking, a field in which there is no turning back.

Company boards should be sensitive to innovation and technological progress, encourage companies to explore, value creativity at all levels, remove red tape from the company culture and stimulate the entrepreneurial spirit.

CONCLUSION

We have tried to explain the swift and far-reaching process of change in the role of company boards and of individual directors against a background of technological innovation, globalization and the growing pace of business.

We have identified a number of gaps and weak spots, such as the absence of good corporate governance in many small and medium-sized companies and the need to reform and constantly update the workings of company boards.

We have considered the role of women on company boards – not because women think differently, but because there is a powerful rise in the number of highly qualified women who are ready to take on board positions.

We have also discussed the need to professionalize company boards, which entails ongoing training, recruitment of internationally experienced directors and better information for the board about the company and its industry. The theme of corporate governance is clearly on the rise in the business world and demands the attention of business owners, whether they are shareholders, large investors, families, or business angels. The most powerful concerns are the need to encourage and support ethical conduct, values, and social responsibility and ensure strict compliance with the law.

We have also explained that, in the context of a society made up of increasingly qualified and skilled individuals, the latter stages of a successful business career may involve a combination of taking up directorships and investing as a business angel. This approach – business angel sponsorship and board-level roles – gives something back to the community, in the form of willingness to invest and to contribute knowledge and expertise.

NOTES

[1] Alfred P Sloan Jr. *My Years with General Motors.* New York: Macfadden-Bartell Corporation; 1963.

[2] Ralph M Hower. *History of Macy's of New York.* Cambridge, Massachusetts: Harvard University Press; 1943.

[3] Jay W Lorsch (ed). *The Future of Boards.* Boston: Harvard Business Review Press; 2012.

[4] Charles P Cotton. *Manual of Railway Engineering.* London: E & FN Spon; 1874.

[5] Clayton M Christensen. *The Innovator's Dilemma.* Boston: Harvard Business Review Press; 2000.

[6] Ram Charan. *Boards that Deliver.* San Francisco: Jossey-Bass; 2005.

[7] Michael Garo. *Step by step to Super Rich.* US: Michael Garo; 2008.

[8] Jeffrey A Sonnenfeld. *What Makes Great Boards Great.* Boston: Harvard Business School Publishing; 2002.

[9] Marc J Epstein, F Warren McFarlan. *Joining a Nonprofit Board.* San Francisco: Jossey-Bass; 2011.

[10] Amy Schuman, Stacy Stutz, John L Ward. *Las Paradojas de la Empresa Familiar.* Barcelona: Deusto; 2013.

[11] Miguel A. Gallo. *La Empresa Familiar: Consejos de Administración.* Barcelona; Estudios y Ediciones IESE, 2001.

[12] Paloma Fernández. *La Profesionalización de las Empresas Familiares.* Madrid: Lid Editorial Empresarial; 2013.

[13] John L Ward. *How Family Values and Vision Drive Business Strategy and Continuity.* In: Josep Tapies, Empresa Familiar: Un Enfoque Multidisciplinar. Spain: Universia; 2011.

[14] María Fernández-Moya, Rafael Castro-Balaguer. *Looking for the Perfect Structure: The Evolution of Family Office From a Long-Term Perspective.* In: Josep Tapies, Empresa Familiar: Un Enfoque Multidisciplinar. Spain: Universia, 2011.

[15] Josep Tapies. *Familia Empresaria.* Madrid: Lid Editorial Empresarial, 2011.

[16] Jordi Canals. *The Future of Leadership Development.* London: Palgrave Macmillan; 2011.

[17] Jordi Canals. *Leadership Development in a Global World.* London: Palgrave Macmillan; 2012

AN INTRODUCTION TO
PEDRO NUENO

Pedro Nueno is a technical architect, industrial engineer and doctor of business administration from Harvard University. He is also Professor of Entrepreneurship at IESE and Chengwei Ventures Chair on Entrepreneurship at CEIBS.

He is the founder and current president of the China Europe International Business School (CEIBS), a leading school of business in Asia, with campuses in Shanghai, Beijing, Shenzhen, Accra and Zurich.

He was a member of the visiting committee of the Harvard Business School, a supervisory board in practice, for six years (2005-2011).

Professor Nueno is also founder of FINAVES, a venture capital corporation associated with the entrepreneurship activity of IESE alumni, which supported the launch of more than 40 companies, creating directly more than 3,000 new jobs. His areas of interest include entrepreneurship, starting new ventures, global management, management of technology, and innovation.

He has authored 14 books translated in several languages about corporate turnaround, innovation, and entrepreneurship.

He has received many honors, such as the Cross of Saint Jordi (2003), the Outstanding Contribution Award from the Chinese government (2014) and "Commander by Number or the Order of Queen Elizabeth the Catholic" (2015).

BEYOND THE WRITTEN WORD

AUTHORS WHO ARE EXPERTS

LID Speakers are proven leaders in current business thinking. Our experienced authors will help you create an engaging and thought-provoking event.

A speakers bureau that is backed up by the expertise of an established business book publisher.

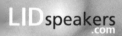

Printed in Great Britain
by Amazon

5449456 9R00051